DOMESTIC VIOLENCE 2000

An Integrated Skills Program for Men

by the same author

THE ADOLESCENT SELF
The Advanced PRISM Workbook

A Norton Professional Book

DOMESTIC VIOLENCE 2000
An Integrated Skills Program for Men

GROUP LEADER'S MANUAL

David B. Wexler, Ph.D.

Relationship Violence Training Institute, San Diego

W. W. NORTON & COMPANY
New York   London

Dr. Wexler is the Director of the Relationship Violence Training Institute in San Diego. He may be reached at

4036 Third Ave.
San Diego, CA 92103
619-296-8103
dbwexler@home.com

For information about permission to reproduce selections
from this book, write to
Permissions, W. W. Norton & Company, Inc., 500 Fifth Avenue,
New York, NY 10110

Composition by PRD Group
Manufacturing by Hamilton Printing

Library of Congress Cataloging-in-Publication Data

Wexler, David B., 1953–
    Domestic violence 2000 : an integrated skills program for men:
men's group leader manual / David B. Wexler.
        p.   cm.
    Includes bibliographical references.
    ISBN 0-393-70314-2
    1. Wife abuse—Prevention Handbooks, manuals, etc.   2. Abusive
men—Rehabilitation Handbooks, manuals, etc.   3. Group psychotherapy
Handbooks, manuals, etc.   I. Title.
HV6626.W44   1999
362.82′927—dc21   99-31249   CIP

W. W. Norton & Company, Inc., 500 Fifth Avenue, New York, N.Y. 10110
www.wwwnorton.com

W. W. Norton & Company Ltd., 10 Coptic Street, London WC1A 1PU

1 2 3 4 5 6 7 8 9 0

To my son, Joseph

Contents

Acknowledgments   xi
Introduction   xiii

Foundations   *1*

Clinical Tips   3
The Broken Mirror: A Self Psychological Perspective for Relationship Violence   6
Feminist, Cognitive, and Behavioral Group Interventions, for Men Who Batter:
  An Overview of Rationale and Method by Daniel G. Saunders, Ph.D.   21
Standard Forms   33
   Weekly Check-in   35
   Group Progress Note   36
   Evaluation Form   37
   Men's Group Orientation   38

Brief Interventions   *41*

1. House of Abuse   43
2. Time-out   50
3. Anger, Aggression, and Red Flags   59
4. Cycles of Abuse   64

Self-Management   *69*

5. Alcohol and Other Substances: What's the Connection?   71
6. Self-talk and Bad Rap   76
7. Using Self-talk for Anger   81
8. Self-esteem   86
9. Feelings: Proper Care and Feeding   90
10. Masculinity Traps I   94
11. Masculinity Traps II   97
12. Jealousy and Misinterpretations   101
13. Put-downs   106
14. Accountability   109

15. Switch!   112
16. Skills Integration   117

Relationship Skills   *119*

17. Assertiveness   121
18. Expressing Feelings and Asking for Change   126
19. Handling Criticism   130
20. Expressing Feelings and Active Listening   136
21. Empathy Training: What My Partner Feels   141
22. The Four Horsemen of the Apocalypse   143
23. Compliments: Giving and Receiving   149
24. Conflict with Respect and Problem-solving   152
25. Expectations of Marriage: Old and New   158
26. Sex   162
27. Kids   169
28. Parents   174

Relapse Prevention   *181*

29-30. Most Violent and/or Most Frightening Incident   183
31. Prevention Plan I   185
32. Prevention Plan II   188

References   193

Index   197

Handouts

Weekly Check-in   35
Group Progress Note   36
Evaluation Form   37
Men's Group Orientation   38

1. The House of Abuse   47
   Emotional Abuse and Mind Games   48
2. The Nine Commandments   53
   Time-out   54
   Time-out Information for Partners   55
   When Your Partner Blocks Your Path   57
   Responsibility Plan   58
3. Understanding Anger   61
   Appropriate Alternatives to Violence   63
4. The Cycle of Abuse   66
5. Alcohol and Other Substances and Abuse: What's the Connection?   73
   Alcohol and Other Substances Questionnaire   74
   Why Do I Use?   75
6. Bad Rap   78
   Bad Rap Quiz   79
   Examples of Anger Producing Self-talk   80
7. HEALS   83
   Self-talk for Anger Management   84
   Anger Ladder   85
8. House of Self-Worth and Empowerment   89
9. The Feelings List   92
   The Cycle of Intolerable Feelings   93
10. Masculinity Traps   96
11. Men Are Supposed to . . .   99
    Rights as a Man   100
12. Jealousy: Taming the Green-eyed Monster   103
    Misinterpretations   105
13. Put-downs from Parents   108
14. Accountability Defenses   110
    Accountability Statement   111

15. Dangerous Self-talk   114
    Confident Self-talk   115
    Switch!   116
16. Joe's Self-talk   118
17. Assertiveness   123
    What Is Assertive Behavior   124
    Keeping Track   125
18. Requests and Refusals   128
    "I" Messages or Asking for Change   129
19. Handling Criticism   132
20. Expressing Your Feelings   138
    Active Listening   139
22. The Four Horsemen of the Apocalypse   145
    Darren & Karen   147
    Repair Mechanisms   148
23. Dealing with Compliments   151
24. Conflict with Respect   154
    Problem-solving   155
    Who Decides?   156
    Expectations of Marriage   157
25. Power and Control Wheel   160
    Equality Wheel   161
26. Sexual Abuse: Psychological and Physical   164
    Masculinity Traps: Sex   165
    Sexual Meaning Questionnaire   166
    I Raped My Wife   167
27. When Kids See Their Parents Fight   171
    Questions for Kids   172
    Kid Stories   173
28. Listening to Kids   176
    Tips for Parents and Kids   177
    Selecting the Right Approach   179
31. Prevention Plan   187
32. Transfer of Change   190

Acknowledgments

Many of the materials in this manual were developed as part of a research project evaluating the efficacy of domestic violence treatment programs co-sponsored by the Department of the Navy and the National Institute of Mental Health. The research was conducted by a team from the University of Colorado, headed by principal investigator Frank Dunford, Ph.D., of the University of Colorado, who offered sage counsel and impeccable support to the fine-tuning of this program.

The constant support and leadership of Sandra Rosswork, Ph.D., the Director of the Navy Family Advocacy Program worldwide, have been invaluable. The support and contributions of Lt. Pamela Murphy, the Director of the Navy Family Advocacy Center in San Diego at the time of the development of the manual, and of Lt. Commander Elizabeth Burns, the Director of the Family Advocacy Center in San Diego during much of the creation and implementation of the curriculum, were essential to the successful development of the Men's Group program. Lt. Commander N. G. "Cindy" Jones also has offered very valuable support to our program development.

Daniel G. Saunders, Ph.D., has been a primary consultant and contributor to this treatment program from the outset. Much of the structure and many of the specific guidelines and exercises in this manual directly originate from him. Some of his specific contributions are noted in the text, in particular the chapter on "Feminist, Cognitive, and Behavioral Group Interventions for Men Who Batter," but many of his informal contributions are not. He has brought vast experience in the field of domestic violence and the highest standards of professionalism to our programs and this manual. I would also like to thank Sue Cramer, L.C.S.W., Joan Tierney, L.C.S.W., and Allen Pluth, Ph.D. for years of valuable collaborations.

James A. Reavis, Psy.D., has also offered significant contributions, based especially on his skills in guiding group members into deeper levels of personal discussions. Robert Geffner, Ph.D., also contributed to the development of many of these materials.

The Family Violence Prevention Fund has graciously allowed us to adapt several pages of their materials from *Domestic Violence: A National Curriculum for Family Preservation Practitioners,* by Susan Schechter and Anne L. Ganley, Ph.D.

I would also like to thank the clinical staff of the Relationship Violence Training Institute, who have been providing outstanding clinical services for the Navy Family Advocacy Center in San Diego since 1986. Their contributions to the program and to the refinement of this manual have been outstanding. These staff members include the following: Cindy Barton, L.C.S.W., Gene Batalia, L.C.S.W., Margaret Bouher, L.C.S.W., Bob Bray, Ph.D., Ana DeSoto, Ph.D., Jerry Gold, Ph.D., Valinda Greene, Ph.D., Delores Jacobs, Ph.D., Christine Kennedy, Ph.D., Michelle Koonin, L.C.S.W., Patricia Landis, Ph.D., Leslie Lotina, L.C.S.W., Mitch Luftig, Ph.D., Ken Marlow, L.C.S.W., James Reavis, Psy.D., Toni Salkas, L.C.S.W., Sheila Stittiams, L.C.S.W., Paul Sussman, Ph.D., Steve Tess, Ph.D., and Christauria Welland-Akong, M.A.

I would also like to thank Susan Munro, my editor, for her belief in this project and for her consistently astute eye and judgment.

The San Diego Domestic Violence Council, and the coordinated community efforts of city attorney, district attorney, police department, judges, community agencies, and victim support groups, have provided an extremely fertile climate for the development of these ideas.

Finally, thanks to all the men who have given so much of themselves and worked so hard throughout our years of treatment. We have found that domestic violence perpetrators come in many shapes and sizes that each man has a unique story to tell.

Introduction

The DOMESTIC VIOLENCE 2000 program integrates elements from profeminist, cognitive-behavioral, and self psychological models for treating domestic violence. The program format and message insist that men examine the dominance and control aspects of domestic violence—especially issues of male entitlement and privilege. It offers men intensive training in new skills for self-management, communication, problem-solving, and empathy for others. And group counselors consistently employ a self psychological, client-centered approach that emphasizes respect for the men's experience—both in personal history and in present relationships—and empathic understanding of why men choose to act the way that they do. The approach is political, educational, and psychological. This model had been carefully constructed through a long process of trial-and-error and through paying attention to input from new research in the field.

OPEN-ENDED vs. CLOSE-ENDED: This manual was originally designed for use in a 32-week program in which all group members begin and end at the same session. However, many groups, for a multitude of reasons, choose not to or are unable to follow this format. The program can easily be adapted to an open-ended group format by utilizing all existing sessions except for Session 1, the Time-Out and Nine Commandments materials from Session 2, the Relapse Prevention materials from Sessions 31 and 32, and the Most Violent Incident exercises from Sessions 29 and 30. The key information in these sessions should be reviewed when a new member enters the group or when one is graduating.

LONGER PROGRAMS: Many programs throughout the country utilize a 52-week treatment format. There are two ways to use this treatment manual in a longer program:

- Many of the session formats are easily expandable into two or more sessions, allowing reviews of the material and personal discussion in greater depth.
- The 32-session format can be reduced to a 26-session format by removing Sessions 1, 2, 29, 30, 31, and 32. The 26 sessions can begin again, so that each group member will go through two cycles of the entire program. The introductory sessions can be reviewed briefly when new group members enter, and the central material from the final four review sessions can be integrated whenever group members graduate.

SHORTER PROGRAMS: For programs that are shorter than 32 sessions, the most important sessions should be selected and used.

STANDARD FORMS: We have included several standard forms for use in the programs. Each form may be used as is, adapted for the needs of the particular program, or abandoned completely. The key forms are:

- Weekly Check-in
- Group Progress Note
- Evaluation Form
- Men's Group Orientation

LIMITATIONS: Many aspects of conducting a comprehensive domestic violence treatment program are <u>not</u> included in this manual: supporting victims, intake and assessment procedures, dealing with fee arrangements, coordinating efforts with court systems and other agencies, selecting and supervising staff members, etc. *We strongly recommend that agencies develop thorough systems and policies for the wider range of services in treating domestic violence.* This manual is designed only to treat heterosexual men who have committed some form of psychological and/or physical act or acts of abuse against their partners. However, the manual has been easily adapted for use with female perpetrators, gay and lesbian perpetrators, adolescent perpetrators, and other populations.

VIDEOTAPES and AUDIOTAPES: Three different videos are used in many of the sessions:

- *Compassion* is available for purchase from Intermedia (1-800-553-8336)
- *The Great Santini* is available for purchase from many video outlets.
  - Scene I (high school basketball game; begin at 1:03:22 and end at 1:12:18)
  - Scene II (father-son one-on-one basketball game; begin at 31:48 and end at 40:23)
  - Scene III (father/mother expressing feelings; begin at 48:23 and end at 54:05
  - Scene IV (kids witnessing spouse abuse; begin at 1:28:29 and end at 1:29:57
- *Men's Work* is available from the Hazelden Foundation (1-800-328-9000)
  - Scene I (series of put downs and masculinity challenges; begin at 2:07 and end at 11:57)
  - Scene II (spouse abuse over dinner/intervention from neighbor; begin at 19:16 and end at 23:42)

The exact timing of the specific video clips from *The Great Santini* and *Men's Work* may be slightly different on different videocassette recorders.

The relaxation audiotapes, *Quieting Reflex, Brief Quieting Reflex,* and *Anger Ladder,* are included with the book or may be purchased from W.W. Norton. Similar relaxation tapes or exercises may be substituted.

RESOURCES FOR MEN: The group members in this program use *DV2000 Resources for Men,* which includes all of the forms marked "Handout" and a set of homework assignments for most of the 32 sessions. These materials are presented in a packet for each member. The forms are three-hole punched for use in a personal binder. The session assignments are purposely not numbered so that individual programs can adjust these materials for their own format. *DV2000 Resources for Men* is available for purchase from W.W. Norton. Discounts are available for group purchases. Please note that these materials are copyrighted and may not be photocopied.

DOMESTIC VIOLENCE 2000

An Integrated Skills Program for Men

FOUNDATIONS

CLINICAL TIPS

The following guidelines are important to keep in mind throughout treatment.

1. **RESPECT:** It is often difficult for clinicians to listen to the stories of the men in our program dispassionately and compassionately. We all enter this setting with our own values and judgments—let alone personal experiences—and the process of understanding a man who abuses his partner can provoke difficult emotions.

   The men in this program deserve our respect—not, obviously, for the actions they have taken, but rather for the individual stories that have led them to act desperately and destructively. It is very helpful to recognize that many of the men in our groups—like all of us—have become overwhelmed by emotions that they had difficulty handling. And they have lacked the necessary range of skills to handle these emotions in constructive and proactive ways. Although we must always emphasize personal responsibility, it is also essential to recognize our essential similarity and their essential humanity.

   It is our belief that when these men become smarter about themselves (more aware of needs, feelings, and motivations) and smarter about options (better skills at self-talk, relaxation, communication, empathy, and problem-solving), they will choose otherwise in the future.

2. **PACING AND LEADING:** One clinical strategy to help facilitate these goals is called "pacing and leading." Originally developed from the work of Milton Erickson, this clinical approach employs the process of carefully mirroring the experience of the other person—followed by a "leading" suggestion for a new way to think or act.

   In our groups, "pacing" means carefully reflecting back an understanding of the men's experience: *You must have felt like everything was spinning completely out of control when Julia confronted you about your drinking. Here she is, holding the baby, telling you to leave until you could get yourself sober. And all you could think of was that she was taking everything away from you—including the baby! And you felt scared, and very powerless, and ashamed all at once. And then you felt like you had to do something to get things back in control. Right then, it must have seemed like nothing else mattered besides making her stay. You could feel yourself getting hot and your muscles getting all charged up. So you lashed out at her, and she fell with the baby in her arms.*

   Then, and only then comes the "lead": *But Chris, I know you, and I know you are not the type of person who wishes harm on your baby or on your wife. I know you can find a way so you won't do something that goes so much against your basic values. This is the time to take a "time out" and use your self-talk: I do not want to hurt my family. . . . I do not want to hurt my family. . . ."* Chris looked down and started crying. *"It's true."* This sequence of communicating empathic understanding and respect for the man's experience, followed by a new perspective or idea proves very valuable in these groups.

3. **INITIAL RESISTANCE:** Very frequently group members enter the first group session angry and resistant. They complain about being in the group, challenge the group policies, and insist that they will not be talking in these sessions. Unless they are seriously disruptive to the group, it is usually best to respectfully listen to their complaints and then move on. **Power struggles should be avoided whenever possible.** Often men who are the most difficult in the early sessions turn out to be the best group members—as long as they have felt respected.

4. **TAKING THINGS SERIOUSLY:** Often, the group members will become uncomfortable with the emotionally disturbing discussions that emerge in the group—and they deal with this by laughing or making fun. Sometimes this happens when a group member describes some act of violence toward his wife or partner that he delivered because she was nagging him so much. It can get tiring for the group leaders to "lecture" the group about how "this is not a funny subject." Often, modeling has the most impact. The group leaders should simply maintain a serious tone themselves. The group members usually get the message quickly. Many of these men are surprisingly sensitive to social cues about correct behavior and they don't want to "look bad."

5. **THE NINE COMMANDMENTS:** The Nine Commandments (see Session 2) are central themes that run through all the treatment sessions, even if there are no specific lectures devoted to them. A poster-size version of these Commandments hangs on the group walls. Whenever a subject related to any of the Commandments emerges in the group discussion, it is helpful to interrupt, point to the poster, and ask someone to read aloud the relevant Commandment.

6. **MALE AND FEMALE COTHERAPISTS:** The optimal format for leading the groups involves a male and female cotherapist team. The group members benefit from a clinical relationship with therapists of both genders. We have generally found it valuable for the <u>male</u> cotherapist to take the lead when confronting any group members regarding female-bashing or negative generalizations about women. This models a different male consciousness about male-female politics—which sounds different when a female appears to be merely defending herself or her gender. Some cotherapist teams choose to handle this differently, because the female may feel patronized by having the male defend her. The cotherapist team can also effectively model respectful disagreement and conflict resolution.

7. **WOMEN-BASHING:** Women-bashing often occurs in these group sessions. This should be confronted **immediately.** Group leaders should point out that generalizations about any social group always turn people into categories rather than individuals. It should be emphasized that *it's OK to say that your wife complains a lot, but not to say that all women are nags.* Furthermore, men who refer to their wife as "the wife" or "she" or even "my wife" should be consistently

asked to refer to her <u>by name.</u> It can be humanizing to write the name of each of the "women" in the group on the board as their names come up during each session. Our goal is to make the women in these men's lives as real and human as possible.

8. **SYSTEM-BASHING:** System-bashing also occurs frequently in the groups: bashing the court system, Child Protective Services, child custody laws, etc. These discussions should be short-circuited as quickly as possible. Unlike women-bashing, however, it is rarely effective to confront these complaints. For one thing, the men may be justified in their complaints. For another, it is unproductive to engage in any unnecessary power struggles. The most effective strategy seems to be saying something like this: *You know, you may be right about some of your complaints, but this isn't really the focus of the group sessions. What we need to talk about here is the things you can do differently in your lives.*

9. **TREATMENT FAILURE:** If any group member is showing clear signs that treatment is not progressing successfully, he should be confronted about his behavior and informed that there is a problem as early as possible in the treatment program. We usually expect to be able to flag these problems by week 6 or 7. It is unfair to inform a group member after 18 sessions that we have decided he is not benefiting from the program (unless some unexpected event, like a re-abuse, has suddenly taken place). Indications of treatment failure include belligerent attitudes, refusal to do any homework, refusal to participate, consistent verbal aggression when discussing females, etc.

10. **POWERLESSNESS:** Although it is obvious that dominance and control are central themes for many of the male domestic violence perpetrators, it is also important to recognize how *powerless* many of these men feel. When we can identify this experience of powerlessness, many of these men are much more accessible to us. They feel less blamed as bad people and more understood as men who have been frustrated or have felt wounded. **It is quite possible to communicate this message without absolving men of responsibility for their abusive actions.**

11. **THERAPIST SELF-DISCLOSURE:** Therapist self-disclosure, in moderation, can be very effective in these treatment groups. Therapists have often created an atmosphere of increased trust and intimacy by acknowledging that some of the same struggles and conflicts have taken place in their own relationships. This is a very valuable tool in helping the group members normalize their experiences, and often enables them to react <u>less</u> explosively to family and personal frustrations.

12. **LIMITATIONS:** When introducing new skills, such as Assertiveness, to the group members, it is very important to emphasize that there is no guarantee that these skills will always bring about a positive outcome. In fact, there are times when being "assertive" or using "active listening" or "I-messages" is not the best course. The message we should send is that usually these are the most *respectful* forms of communication, and *respectful* communication is generally the most effective in the long run.

THE BROKEN MIRROR:
A Self Psychological Treatment Perspective for Relationship Violence

The first four to six months we were together, I thought I was just walking on water. Everything I did was wonderful. Everything about me was cool. I felt great. It was almost like I looked at her and I would always feel great about myself. And then it all came crashing down. She doesn't look at me the same way anymore. The kids demand a lot of attention. It's like she doesn't think I'm that great anymore. So now, I don't even talk to her about a lot of things because they might upset her and mess up her picture of me even more—even when I know that she'll get even madder at me later for lying to her. And then I get mad at her, like it's her fault that I don't feel like I walk on water any more!

One time my son, when he was nine, was trying to do this bike stunt where he would have to make his bike jump in the air and then come down over some boards. He couldn't do it. He was scared. I really got on him: "You're a baby, you're chicken, you're weak. I'm going to take your bike away from you!" I kept thinking he was letting me down! It was like he was disrespecting me.

When a man comes home to his wife and children, he expects that something will take place in the transaction between them that will offer him a state of emotional well-being, or what is referred to in self psychology as a state of self-cohesion. The need for self-cohesion is primary. Its origins lie in the original needs between the infant or young child and the most central attachment figure, usually the mother. The child has a compelling need to look into the face of his mother and see, reflected back to him, eyes that say "You are wonderful" and a smile that says "You make me happy."

This is his magic mirror, and the figure in the mirror is known in self psychology theory as the mirroring selfobject. The self psychology theory of normal child development (Shapiro, 1995) states that all children, at some point in their development, need validation and acknowledgment from parental figures. Over time, these lead to the child's capacity to feel pride and take pleasure in his or her accomplishments—to feel a sense of competence and efficacy.

Children who are deprived of these essential responses, or who instead are subjected to criticism and ridicule for the efforts to achieve, become arrested in their development of an internal sense of confidence and competence. As adults, they are

Reprinted with permission from *Journal of Psychotherapy Practice and Research,* 8(2), 1999.

always looking to some outside source of approval or recognition (mirroring). But no mother, no father, no teacher, no coach, and no therapist ever provide the perfect mirror. Some of these mirroring figures, as we all know rather too well, are often quite fragmented themselves and have little capacity to offer the loving and self-enhancing reflection that the child desperately requires. Or, in some cases, a mismatch between child and mirror-figure takes place such that the child eternally feels a lack of understanding, a dearth of genuine appreciation, and a fundamental gap in attunement. Even in the best of situations, it can be experienced as incomplete. The child thus develops gaps in his sense of self: he mistrusts and disrespects his own internal signals and states; he doubts his own self-worth and competence. He desperately turns elsewhere for validation and, even more than most of us, he becomes excessively sensitized to signals that might suggest that he is unappreciated, unneeded, or unsuccessful.

Thus, the adult man who has been deprived of these essential mirroring functions turns, unconsciously, to his closest adult relationships and activities to help him acquire what was never soundly established long ago. He enters a love relationship with defenses erected against too much intimacy, for fear of being hurt and missing attunement once again. The needs resurface, inevitably, as the emotional connection develops. He hopes, he prays, that the good feelings he has about himself as he intertwines his life with his partner and family will buoy him for the rest of his life against the emptiness and deprivation that he has already experienced.

Some of this psychology can best be understood from an understanding of the power to generate a state of self-cohesion and well-being that men in our culture frequently offer women. Pleck (1980) outlines two very important dimensions of male reliance on female validation.

The first is that men perceive women as having *expressive power*, the power to express emotions. Many men have learned to depend on women to help them express emotions; in fact, women's richer emotional life and capacity for emotional expression provides an essential life spark for many men. Whether they can identify this or not, many men feel lost without the fundamental connection to this spark.

The second form of reliance is *masculinity-validating* power. Men depend on women to remind them, and reassure them, of their fundamental masculinity and masculine self-worth. When a woman refuses to offer this validation, or when a man's unrealistic expectations and subsequent distortions convince him that she is withholding this, many men feel lost. They desperately demand the restoration of their virility, masculinity, self-worth, and, ultimately, self-cohesion, by the powerful confirming source. Thus, the reflection offered by these female mirrors is extremely powerful. And the man who craves mirroring finds, as the relationship moves on, that his wife, and now his children, and the job he has, and the life they have together have not sufficiently made up for what he has never received. When his wife seems more interested in talking to her sister than to him, and when their sex life wanes, and when his children do not show the respect to their parents that he envisioned, he becomes fragmented. When these responses are not forthcoming, these men are unable to maintain their sense of self-worth, self-esteem, or validity. Various types of behaviors reflecting this fragmentation may ensue (gambling, substance abuse, reckless sexual behavior, aggression, etc.).

White and Weiner (1986) offer a valuable description from the self psychological perspective of the experience of the abusive parent, which is quite parallel to the experience of the frustrated, abusive husband. They identify the narcissistic rage over the inability to *make* the child react as if he or she were part of the parent's self and really know what was wanted. Here, the mirroring selfobject function is extremely important, and quite fragile. So long as a child (or partner) provides the appreciation needed, self-esteem is maintained. When the applause fails, the narcissistic rage erupts along with an inner experience of a fragmenting self. The narcissistically impaired adult needs to be respected and obeyed and made to feel worthwhile; when he does not see that positive reflection in the interpersonal mirror, he is left feeling vulnerable, helpless, and outraged.

I've been married ten years. The first six years were picture perfect. We had little spats, but that was all. But then this thing called parenthood came along. She was more critical of me, plus the heat from my career got way turned up. And she just got more and more of an attitude. And I'm thinking, "You're not the only one entitled to have an attitude." I became the sole breadwinner, and instead of making her an equal partner in our lives, my "father" came out of me.

I just became my dad! Instead of looking at the fact that she was stressed out, I just blew up. Everything that I had said I would never do, I did anyway!

I can drink myself into oblivion just to escape from my feelings. Of course, I can be just as mean sober. I have developed this incredibly painful jaw and neck. It can ruin my night. It has everything to do with all this stress and anger and attitude.

Some disappointment like this is inevitable in the course of human relationships and the recognition of limits. **The problem with the man who becomes abusive with his partner or children is that he has mistaken the flood of good feelings that comes from a close relationship with a promise that the good mirror will always shine.** So, in his eyes, the mirror breaks, his sense of self shatters, and he blames the mirror. **Because she promised.**

Stosny (1995) describes these men as "attachment abusers." When they see reflected back to them an image that makes them feel unlovable or inadequate, they feel ashamed. They blame the mirror for the reflection.

Some of these men become psychologically, sexually, emotionally, and/or physically abusive with their partners—because these psychological vulnerabilities, in combination with other social and environmental factors, set the stage for abusive acts in relationships. Dutton's (Dutton & Golant, 1995) research on the origins of male battering identifies the ways in which socialization combines with psychological influences to create an abusive personality: Contributing factors include a sense of powerlessness in early childhood, the experience of having been shamed and battered, and couples with insecure avoidant-ambivalent bonding styles. Men who scored the highest for "fearful attachment" also scored highest for jealousy. "Jealousy," the authors note, "is the terror of abandonment" (p. 139). They go on to demonstrate that these fears are at the center of many abusive acts.

The treatment implications of this are profound. The clinician who can genuinely understand the perpetrator's unmet needs for mirroring and affirmation—and who can suspend preoccupation with moralistically rejecting the immature and unacceptable forms through which these were expressed—is potentially of tremendous value. The selfobject needs of the perpetrator are *valid.* Recognizing how the behaviors that he chooses are intended to regain self-cohesion and some sense of power and control *over his crumbling sense of self* (not necessarily over *another person*) leads to a new, more accessible, and deeply respectful therapeutic encounter.

If we understand the driving force behind many of these men, we can recognize that most of them (with some notable exceptions, as will be explained below) are not that different from most other men or women. Their actions may violate moral or legal codes and may not be in the behavioral repertoire of many other adults, but the fundamental emotions, needs, and struggles are certainly not unique or foreign. The task of clinicians and educators, in offering treatment, is to understand this pattern and to offer these men a new narrative of themselves and a new set of tools for coping with these very human experiences. The self psychology perspective (Shapiro, 1995; White & Weiner, 1986), which emphasizes the breakdowns in the *experience* of self-cohesion leading to desperate acts, offers us a map.

Typology of Batterers

Before proceeding any further with this particular portrait of the dynamics of the abusive man, it is essential to clarify some of the different typologies that current research has outlined. Johnson (1995) has categorized spousal abuse into two main groups: "patriarchal terrorism" and "common couple violence." The origins, motivations, and patterns are quite different, even if they do have the one central feature of physical aggression or intimidation in an intimate relationship to link them. He is convinced that different researchers in the field have identified quite different descriptions of spousal abuse because they have studied quite different populations: battered women's shelter populations versus overall population samples. "Patriarchal terrorism," based on research from women's shelter populations, is generally the more dangerous of the two. The violence occurs with greater severity and frequency. It is only male-to-female. Men in this category who commit acts of spousal abuse are characterized by a need to be in charge of the relationship and to control the woman by any means necessary. The males in these relationships are determined to maintain a structure of power and control, utilizing the various abusive strategies of physical violence, threats and intimidation, sexual abuse, emotional/verbal/psychological abuse, economic control, and social isolation. They invoke the rights of male privilege and male entitlement.

"Common couple violence," in contrast, is an intermittent response to the occasional conflicts of everyday life, motivated by a need to control a specific situation. The complexities of family life produce conflicts that occasionally get out of hand. The violence is no more likely to be enacted by men than by women. This type of violence, concludes Johnson, is usually not a part of a pattern in which one partner is trying to exert general control over his or her partner. This form of spouse abuse is relatively nongendered.

The heart of the difference between these two types of family violence lies in the motivation. While patriarchal terrorism assumes that the violent behaviors represent the larger context of male power and control, male entitlement, and male dominance, common couple violence stems from a less specific purpose. The intent with this type of violence is not specifically to control the partner, but more to express frustration. Similarly, Prince and Arias (1994) identified two sets of men, one which seemed to use violence that is consistent with their personal preferences and convictions and the other for whom violence seemed to be a result of frustration—an expressive, misguided cathartic response. These distinctions have otherwise been described as "chronic batterers vs. sporadic batterers" or, simply, "battering vs. physical violence." Battering is physical aggression with a purpose: to control, intimidate, or subjugate another person. It is *always* accompanied by psychological abuse. Many other acts of physical and/or psychological abuse may be designed to gain power and control in that specific situation, but they do not always represent a systematic pattern for that purpose.

MALE SPOUSE ABUSER SUBTYPES

As in most other clinical populations, researchers cannot exactly agree on the typologies of men who commit acts of domestic violence. However, several different leading researchers have developed basic categories, which generally overlap. In a review of the literature, Holtzworth-Munroe and Stuart (1994) found that the research pointed to three main categories. I will refer to these categories as Type I, Type II, and Type III. Type I batterers are generally antisocial and more likely to engage in instrumental violence. Aggression "works" more successfully for them. They are limited in their capacity for empathy and attachment, and they hold the most rigid and conservative attitudes about women. They tend to be violent across situations and across different victims. They are more generally belligerent, more likely to abuse substances, and more likely to have a criminal history. They show little remorse. Surprisingly, they report low to moderate levels of anger.

There is a certain population of battering or otherwise abusive men for whom the model of the broken mirror does not particularly apply, and for whom practically any treatment intervention appears quite unlikely to be successful. These are men who are now described as "vagal reactors" or "cobras" (Jacobson & Gottman, 1998b) or, by some descriptions, psychopaths (Hare, 1993). Psychophysiologically-based studies by Gottman and colleagues (Gottman et al., 1995; Jacobson & Gottman, 1998b) identified an unusual pattern among a subgroup of the most severe batterers, who actually showed a reduction in measures of arousal during aggressive interactions with their partners—completely contrary to expectations and typical patterns during angry interactions. These researchers have identified these men as "vagal reactors" whose nervous system arousal is strangely disconnected from their behavior. These batterers are deliberately, manipulatively controlling what goes on in the marital interaction. Men who operate in this cold and calculating manner probably cannot be reached through treatment, at least treatment as we now know it. Jacobson and Gottman (1998b) call these men "cobras" because of their ability to become still and focused before striking their victim—in contrast to the more typical "pit bulls" who do a slow burn in frustration and resentment before finally exploding. They display many of the characteristics of classic psychopathic behavior—not necessarily typical of all Type I abusers.

Type II batterers are described by several researchers as "family-only." They are dependent and jealous. They tend to suppress emotions and withdraw, later erupting into violence after long periods of unexpressed but seething rage. They tend to commit acts of abuse only in the family. Their acts of abuse are generally less severe, and they are less aggressive in general. They are generally remorseful about their actions.

> *I suddenly realized that I had been through five years of not communicating anything to her! Then it all exploded over the fish tank. My fish tank was really important to me. This was not just a little goldfish bowl—it was my 50-gallon aquarium that I had put a lot of work into. And I was ready to find a place for it in our house. So—trying to be polite about it—I said to her, "Well, where do you think it should go?" and she just explodes with that nasty tone, "I don't care where the fucking fish tank goes!" And I lost it. I pretended to grab a razor blade and wave it around. To show her how shitty I felt. She threw a hanger at me. I grabbed her, pushed her onto the ground. I didn't even know what I was doing. I started choking her and the next thing I knew she was gasping for breath and I eased up. I couldn't remember anything at first, and then it all came back to me. My self-talk? It's not fair. . . . She's disrespecting me. . . . She doesn't care about me. . .*

. I've been holding this in for so long, now it's finally her turn to hear about it!
And I kind of woke up and looked around. "What the hell have I done?"

Type III batterers are usually identified as "dysphoric/borderline" or "emotionally volatile." They tend to be violent only within their family, but they are more socially isolated and socially incompetent than other batterers. They exhibit the highest levels of anger, depression, and jealousy. They find ways of misinterpreting their partners and blaming their partners for their own mood states. Depression and feelings of inadequacy are prominent. They are more likely to have schizoid or borderline personalities.

> I had broken up with Danielle months ago. And I was screwing around with a couple of different girls at this point. But I still couldn't get her out of my head. A friend of mine told me that he had heard Danielle was dancing again in strip clubs because she was so broke. I went nuts. I stormed over to her place and I started fucking screaming at her: "I AM GONNA DISFIGURE YOUR WHOLE BODY IF I EVER FIND OUT YOU ARE DANCING AGAIN!" I'm not really gonna do it, but I felt like it.
>
> When I picture her dancing or having sex with another guy who doesn't have the utmost dignity and respect for her, I just want to kill her!
>
> That girl gave me more than anybody in my life. She would do anything for me. She would fly to fucking Australia to bring me a sweater if I was cold. She was like my mother.
>
> I just get in so much pain—where I need to find her. Last night I got hit with this wave of missing her and I went all over looking for her. I know it's not right.
>
> But I feel like if I could just see her, she'd be with me, the bad feelings would go away, and everything would be OK. I wouldn't have to worry anymore.

So it appears that a small percentage of the most severe batterers are beyond the reach of clinical and/or psychoeducational interventions, suited only for external consequences as possible controls on behavior. In fact, many of these more severely dangerous men (the "cobras," the psychopathic men, the severely antisocial) do not ever make it into the treatment system: some may be in jail for other crimes, others slickly escape detection altogether, and still others somehow manage to avoid fulfilling court-ordered treatment requirements. But the encouraging findings are that so many other men in this population are not beyond our reach. They share a kinship with men and women who are not spouse abusers, and our understanding of fundamental psychological principles combined with the influence of cultural models of violence bring them within the realm of clinical connection.

SHAME

Dutton's model (Dutton & Golant, 1995) for understanding the multiple factors which set the stage for domestic violence is particularly illuminating about the male psychological experience. And it especially allows us to develop a more empathic understanding of these men. Dutton outlined several key background factors that set the stage for a boy growing up to become a man who batters. Although this paradigm was developed based on studies of only one category (emotionally volatile/Type III), the principles significantly overlap into the other categories as well. Dutton explains how the seeds come from three distinct sources: being shamed (especially by one's father), an insecure attachment to one's mother, and the direct observation of abusiveness in the home.

According to Dutton, shaming comes from public exposure of one's vulnerability. The whole self feels "bad." Abused children often shut off all emotion, to defend against rage and hurt at perpetrator. A father who shames has a need to punish. When he attacks his son, he is desperately attempting to regain some lost sense of self, to bolster or reassure his own shaky sense of self. For the boy who needs to feel loved by this main source of his male identity, it is a series of crushing blows.

> *My father used to put me down. He slapped me around, called me "shit for brains," told me he should have never had me. Now I get it. When my wife says something that sounds even a little bit critical, I hear the same damn thing in my head: "shit for brains, shit for brains . . ."*
>
> *If I stacked something wrong in the store, he'd slap me upside the head in front of other people. He would call me stupid. I was always nervous about the type of job I was doing. He would slap me if I screwed up until I got it right.*
>
> *I was a good enough athlete to play college ball in three sports—but he would always criticize me. I once got a whipping for not winning a race–he thought I hadn't put out full effort. The way my father brought me up caused me more problems. I'm not satisfied with who I am and I never will be.*

People who have been exposed to shame will do anything to avoid it in the future. They develop a hypersensitive radar to the possibility of humiliation, and they are almost phobic in their overreactivity. They tend to project blame and perceive the worst in others. These men are, tragically, usually the ones most desperate for affection and approval but they cannot ask for it. Sometimes the smallest signs of withdrawal of affection will activate the old narcissistic wounds—and they lash out at the perceived source of this new wound. They can describe none of these feelings; they don't even know where they have come from.

Furthermore, if the mother of this young child is only intermittently capable of offering emotional connection and support, he spends too much time trying to bring her closer; this drains him of the attention, energy, and confidence needed for moving forward developmentally. Conversely, if she is too anxious and needs too much attention or validation from *him,* she intrudes upon him and he cannot separate. He never fully develops an inner sense of a lovable, stable, valuable core self. This boy develops an ambivalent attitude toward her and later toward women in general: they are the providers of essential emotional life-support, but they are only intermittently trustworthy and available.

As attachment is necessary for survival, the male learns early that his mother (and, by association, any intimate woman) has monumental power over him. True emotional safety and security are initially associated with the physical presence of a woman—but it is only inconsistently available. As adults, these men try to diminish their anxiety about being abandoned by exaggerated control of their female partner.

> *With my wife—she gets on me about moving the furniture, that I'm not doing it right: "You always do this, you never do that, you never think about anyone else, you're only thinking about yourself. . . ." The leg of the sofa breaks, now I'm the dummy who did it. She runs me down about money. But I excel at lots of things, and I seem to get criticized anyway. The minute she gives me any sort of criticism, I get mad enough to fight.*

As Dutton (Dutton & Golant, 1995) describes it, "A boy with an absent or punitive father and a demanding but unavailable mother learns that men don't give emotional comfort, and that women appear to be supportive but are ultimately demanding and can't be trusted" (p. 114).

This is the cry of the little boy within the grown man: "Why can't she make me feel better?"

When these psychological variables are combined with the observation of abusive behavior in the home, we have a future prescription for male relationship violence. Research studies have indicated that males who witnessed parents attacking each other were three-to-four times more likely to eventually assault their wives (Straus, Gelles, & Steinmetz, 1980). Although being on the receiving end of physical and emotional abuse is a prominent variable in the population of spouse abusers, witnessing male-female adult abuse is even more significant (Hotaling & Sugarman, 1986; Kalmuss, 1984).

Evolution of Treatment Approaches

Advocates of the "power and control"-based interventions, the approaches Johnson refers to as based on theories of patriarchal terrorism, describe their treatment as educational—in fact, not as "treatment" at all, if "treatment" implies "therapeutic" (Pence & Paymar, 1993). The "Duluth" model is the most prominent model advocating this approach, and the dominance of this model is most clearly evident by the fact that many state legislatures, including California's, have dictated that only programs based on this model can be used by court-approved treatment providers. Even programs that have developed a more integrated cognitive-behavioral approach have included major philosophical components of the Duluth model. The goal of this model is the reeducation of men in their use of power, male privilege, and male entitlement in their relationships with women. Based on the sociocultural, feminist perspective of male patriarchy and relationship violence, battering is identified as a natural outcome of a society that reinforces male power and dominance. The social norms and attitudes are identified as the central culprit in spousal abuse.

The dominance of programs based on this model grew out of the sociocultural analyses of the 70s and 80s. The interventions—always in groups—were in direct response to the previous dominant clinical intervention style: identify the problem as a relationship dysfunction, work with the couple, identify ways in which both partners contributed to the conflicts, examine the pressures on the perpetrator, focus on how the victim's psychological disturbances would cause her to stay in such a relationship, etc. In contrast, socioculturally-based programs, which held men directly accountable for their actions, removed the stigma from women as having "caused" the violence, and insisted that "men helping men" was the most potent forum in which to examine the fundamental attitudes governing spousal abuse, were a very welcome and valuable addition to the field. In these programs, men were confronted consistently on their denial of abuse, their minimization of the severity of its effects, their rationalizations about how they were provoked, and their blame of external factors for their behavior (alcohol, stress, etc.)

As socioculturally-based programs have proliferated in the 80s and 90s, however, several problems in effectiveness have emerged, and it is this author's belief that many of these criticisms are justified. These programs have been criticized for relying too much on a confrontational style, for only acknowledging male violence and discounting the frequency and significance of female or "bidirectional" violence, and for treating all men who have committed acts of spouse abuse as being motivated by "patriarchal terrorism." As Stosny (Jacobson & Gottman, 1998a) puts it, "Most treatment programs focus on how men's domination causes domestic violence. We say that the real gender variable is that culture doesn't teach men to regulate their negative emotions, or sustain trust, compassion, and love. . . . But you can't [treat domestic violence] with a gender war. . . . By demonizing the batterer, it makes him more isolated" (p. 82). They have also been criticized for not fully emphasizing skill-building and for completely forbidding any couples treatment for any cases. While for the purposes of this paper the differences between the "patriarchal terrorism" treatment approaches and the "common couple violence" are highlighted, in actual practice the interventions originating from both of these camps are often integrated. However, some fundamental philosophical differences emerge that cannot be overlooked.

EFFECTS OF CONFRONTATIONAL APPROACHES

In these approaches, advocated for much of the past decade in treating domestic violence offenders, the focus is always on gender and power issues. All attempts to "psychologize" the problem are confronted as a form of denial or abdication of male responsibility. In this view, the perpetrator should consistently be confronted on rationalization, denial, and victim-blaming. Group members are pushed to admit, from day one, that they have committed violent and abusive acts and to describe these acts in detail without minimization, rationalization, or denial. The analysis of aggression is based primarily on its instrumental value in maintaining power and control in male-female relationships. These approaches are, in many ways, "shame-based," in that men are confronted with their misconduct prior to any establishment of rapport or recognition of the male experience.

In studies of individual psychotherapy, however, Henry, Schacht, and Strupp (1986, 1990) recognized that clients with deeply damaged sense of self-esteem and issues of personal shame (typical of many domestic violence perpetrators) were highly sensitized to negative messages from therapists. They emphasize how introjects—the ways in which people learn to treat themselves as they have been treated by others—help form a relatively stable structure for how an individual treats his or her "self." They found that therapists who consistently offered positive support and positive reframing of client behaviors and who accepted and encouraged client autonomy (who were "affiliative") produced responses from clients which were characterized by increased self-expression and better self-esteem. Much like the control-mastery theory of Weiss and Sampson (1986), they concluded that therapists must find a way to pass the unconscious "tests" of these clients by offering them a different perspective: an experience of acceptance rather than rejection, of respect rather than shame, and of autonomy rather than control.

Murphy and Baxter (1997) reviewed confrontational approaches in treatment settings. They concluded that therapist criticism and aggressive confrontation of client defenses are often counterproductive. Highly empathic therapists are more effective than highly confrontational ones. In reviewing research on rape education programs, Fischer (1986) concluded that confrontational socioculturally-based programs that emphasized the portrayal of men as brutes and women as helpless victims actually decreased the likelihood of success—even leading to undesirable backlash effects. Although the more confrontational approaches appear logical in terms of challenging the distorted cognitions and attitudes, there is many a slip from the cup to the lip between good intentions and good outcome. The crucial clinical variable of offering and modeling respect is often missing in these approaches. "Such practices and attitudes engage the batterer in an old, familiar game of power and control, victim and victimizer, with a temporary turn of the tables" (Murphy & Baxter, 1997, p. 609). When it comes to the values of respectful relationships, not only do treatment providers need to preach them, but they also have to show them. There is a danger of establishing a power hierarchy in the treatment setting that subtly reinforces power tactics—and that alienates the very population we want to reach.

As Dutton (1998) points out, abusive men must not be confronted too strongly or too quickly because of their hypersensitivity to the experience of shame. The more they experience the treatment setting as a forum for increased shame, the more likely they are to defend against this experience by defensive digging in of the heels: intensified anger, rationalization of violence, and projection of blame.

Even if the sociocultural analysis of domestic violence applied to all cases referred for treatment—which it does not—insisting that men recognize (right from the beginning of treatment) that they are representing a male patriarchal culture, that they are engaged in power and control tactics with their partners, and that their partners' violence toward them was strictly an act of self-defense will alienate many of them. Hardening defenses will not serve the men we treat, nor their partners whom we are ultimately trying to protect.

Client-Centered Approaches: Respect

While this chapter is most centrally focused on the self psychology perspective, there are a number of kindred approaches that emphasize similar principles and values. Although these approaches may differ in terms of length of treatment, emphasis on psychoeducational content or use of skill-building techniques, they share the fundamental respect for the male abuser's personal experience. None of these approaches denies the severity of domestic violence, nor do they encourage men to shirk their responsibility. These approaches simply propose a way of making contact with these men so that they are more accessible for changing.

It is also important to point out that these umbrella orientations can be quite compatible with treatment strategies that integrate power and control issues and cognitive-behavioral skills training.

PACING AND LEADING

One clinical approach that transcends the specific theories and programs is based on the clinical strategy of "pacing and leading." This approach, originating from the work of Milton Erickson and further developed by neo-Ericksonian practitioners (Erickson & Rossi, 1979; Gilligan, 1987), carefully mirrors the experience of the other person—followed by a "leading" suggestion for a new way to think or act. Based on Erickson's original work with indirect, naturalistic hypnotherapy, pacing means first developing empathy and rapport for the other person's experience by careful delineation—prior to making any correction or suggestion, prior to fostering a new perspective, prior to guiding a new behavior.

In domestic violence groups, "pacing" means carefully reflecting back an understanding of the men's experience: *When Karen was talking to this other guy at the party, you must have felt really threatened, like something very important was being taken away from you. And you must have felt betrayed, like "How can she do this to me?" Plus it was in front of other people, and your pride was at stake. And you felt powerless, probably thinking that "I have to do something about this right now." You probably felt* *it all through your body, and it felt awful, and you didn't know what to do. It makes sense that you would feel this way, and that you would feel this urge to try to do <u>something</u> to feel powerful again.*

Then, and only then, comes the "lead": *And at that point, probably the most <u>powerful</u> thing to do would be to remember that you get insecure in these situations, and that it doesn't always mean that Karen is <u>doing</u> something to you. And to remember that you have ways to talk to her about it afterwards. You can let her know what you need from her.*

This sequence, of communicating empathic understanding and respect for the man's experience, followed by a new perspective or idea, has a profound impact on preparing the men for new ways of thinking and acting. Saunders (1982) points out that clinicians can be informed by the basic axiom of "accept the client but reject the behavior"; he also points out that, in most cases, one does not need to look very far to find a redeeming feature in each man. Showing an understanding of the man's fear, hurt, sense of helplessness, and anger not only fosters treatment progress, but also defuses the potential for any outbreaks of violence toward the therapist.

Similarly, the "freeze-frame" approach (Wexler, 1991, 1994) is extremely valuable in generating greater accessibility to these men. This approach employs a self psychological perspective in helping men recognize the fundamental—and very "respectable"—emotional needs that they were experiencing at the time that they made the behavioral decision that turned out to have destructive or self-destructive consequences. The primary attention to the genuine experience and legitimate emotional needs (e.g., attention, self-esteem, appreciation, security, self-efficacy, etc.) radically dilutes the potential defensiveness. Based on our experience, the training and corrections that inevitably follow in domestic violence programs are better received.

SELF PSYCHOLOGY APPROACHES: THE SELFOBJECT PERSPECTIVE

Several concepts from self psychology are especially valuable in making sense of the spouse abuser's experience and in guiding treatment interventions. First and foremost is the concept of the mirroring selfobject (Shapiro, 1995; White & Weiner, 1986; Wolf, 1988; Wolfe, 1989). When a child looks into the eyes of his parent and sees reflected back to him a loving and approving look, his basic sense of himself is deeply validated. He feels alive and worthy. When an adult male in a relationship looks into the eyes of his partner and sees reflected back to him a look of love and delight and profound respect, he likewise feels alive and worthy. However, since this perfect mirroring inevitably—even in the best of relationships—wears off, at least to some degree, this man is doomed to a cracking of the mirror and a cracking of the self. It is this experience that must be identified and owned for many men who turn on their partners. They need to understand the origin of their deep unrest and their deep resentment so they can position themselves to possibly take some responsibility for it. As with most other psychological experiences, the identified and known experience has a profound organizing effect and allows the individual to respond more maturely and appropriately to the genuine problem. The twinship selfobject is a much more adaptive experience at this point in the relationship. This would allow a husband to say to his wife, *"Y'know, I feel really lost sometimes without all the special times we had together. It just seems like having kids and getting used to each other and money problems have really taken their toll. I guess you must feel the same way."* Here the man has shifted his primary need from the mirroring function of his partner to one in which they are profoundly alike. She is no longer the enemy, but rather a comrade along the difficult road of life—a comrade who is inevitably flawed, but no more fundamentally flawed than he.

Also from the self psychology perspective, it is important to recognize the fundamental narcissistic injury or selfobject breakdown that usually precedes an outbreak of abusive behavior. In fact, we can usually observe the effects of an injury to the vulnerable self in the clinical relationship, since there is inevitably an empathic failure in all treatment experiences. The research of Holtzworth-Munroe and Hutchinson (1993) is particularly illuminating here. They examined the "misattributions" of men who abuse their wives compared to a non-abusive male population. They found that violent husbands were much more likely to attribute the most negative intentions to their wives' behavior: when presented vignettes of situations like a wife talking to another man at a party or a wife who is not interested in sex on a particular night, these men were much more likely to be convinced that she was *trying* to make the man angry, hurt his feelings, put him down, get something for herself, or pick a fight. The researchers also found that when the men *perceived* a situation of abandonment or rejection, they were particularly likely to generate incompetent behavioral responses. These are narcissistic injuries to these men; and, as with all narcissistic injuries, they are strictly governed by the cognitive interpretation of the event. A nonviolent husband might interpret the same situation in a different, more benign way. If his wife were spending a lot of time talking to another man at a party, he might be irritated at her, or he might make nothing of it, or he might actually feel pleased that she was attractive and popular and having a good time. This recognition of the vulnerability to narcissistic injury—and the ability to communicate this understanding in the clinical setting—allow both us and these men in treatment to develop a greater respect for how their hurt feelings and eventual desperate reactions developed.

The clinical goal here is to create an "experience-near" intervention; with this population, that must elicit the man's experience of being *powerless*, no matter how much the political analysis as observed from outside indicates that he is *powerful*. Harway and Evans (1996) critique one of the foundation pieces of the domestic violence models: Walker's "Cycle of Violence" (Walker, 1984). The original cycle identifies the stages that some spousal battering patterns go through: escalation to explosion to honeymoon period. Both man and woman tend to deny the problems of the other stages because of the sweetness and satisfaction of the honeymoon period—but, tragically, the escalation period inevitably reemerges, culminating in explosion once more. According to Walker, this cycle tends to become shorter and shorter, with more frequent and more disturbing periods of escalation and explosion.

More recent research suggests that many couples do *not* experience this pattern of more rapid cycling and more dangerous intensity (Johnson, 1995). Many couples have occasional incidents of abuse that do not inevitably lead to more danger. And, certainly, many men do not *experience* this cycle in the way that is described. The fact that they do not experience it this way does not invalidate it, but it certainly does not lend itself to being a valuable intervention. To confront men in treatment with the cycle of violence model as *the* quintessential pattern of abuse—with its emphasis on male domination and inevitable escalation—causes us to lose much of our audience. Many of these men do not feel that this accurately describes them and they become defensive or, even worse, disengaged.

Instead, Harway and Evans (1996) use the "Cycle of Feeling Avoidance." This model reflects the more typical—and often surprising—experience of powerlessness that men have in difficult interpersonal relationships. Many men—and certainly many men who become abusive—have very low tolerance for difficult or aversive feelings

(Gottman, 1994). When they experience some personal injury or discomfort, they feel overwhelmed. A mistake may lead to shame, frustration to helplessness, emotional distance to loneliness. In this model, men do *whatever it takes* to defend against these extremely dysphoric states. They may behave with passivity, such as placating or excessive apologizing just to keep the peace. Or they may take a more active approach, as men in our culture are oriented to do: lashing out at the person who seems to be causing this pain, engaging in controlling behavior to eliminate the sources of discomfort, abusing substances as an escape from the feelings, acting out recklessly (such as sexual escapades or dangerous driving) to provide some relief.

> *So here I am, in this kind of frenzy, I guess, pretending to wave this razor blade around. It wasn't even in my hand, but she thought it was. And I can hear this screaming my head: "You don't care about me!" "I want to have control over SOMETHING in my life!" And later I thought about how I had been adopted, and how I didn't even get to "choose" my real parents; they made that decision for me.*

In this state, under these circumstances, the other people in this man's life are perceived *only* as potential selfobject figures. His wife's behavior, feelings, and "independent center of initiative" are peripheral to the fundamental drive for self-cohesion: he will do *anything it takes* to avoid the dysphoria and regain some measure of well-being. Often this means gaining control over someone else. And often this means emotional, verbal, or physical abuse.

In the treatment setting, clinicians can offer these men a new, stable, mirroring selfobject—so that they can feel a deeper sense of self-respect and can maintain a more grounded sense of self as they deal with the emotional minefield inherent in many love relationships. And they can offer them a new, mature twinship experience—so that they can recognize that we are similar passengers on this journey through sensitive episodes and difficult moments in relationships. While many of us would not turn to physically abusive or emotionally intimidating behavior, we at least share the experience of feeling hurt and threatened and occasionally resorting to behaviors in response to these states that we deeply regret. In this way, clinicians and clients can experience twinship.

CLIENT-CENTERED GROUP FORMATS

Some specific group formats have adopted a psychological, client-centered treatment plan that does not include the educational components found in other programs. These programs share a fundamental belief in the individual's ability to heal from childhood wounds, to build on strengths, or both.

Process Psychodynamic Treatment

Saunders (1996b; Browne, Saunders, & Staecker, 1997) developed a model of domestic violence treatment based on a "process/psychodynamic" approach. This is another domestic violence intervention informed by a clinical approach that—again, without absolving men for taking responsibility for their actions—emphasizes the understanding of the perpetrator's experience rather than the confrontation of gender politics and the men's perpetutation of such. This model assumes that men need to grieve their childhood pains and losses in a safe environment. Saunders based the design of this approach on several theories and studies that emphasize the threats and injuries to the sense of self that men experience. Pleck (1980) suggested that men perceive women as being superior in their ability to express themselves—thus, men become dependent on females and turn to them for nurturant and emotional needs. They rely on women to support their sense of masculinity, and therefore *experience* themselves as being powerless compared to their female partner. When women do not meet their perceived needs, they experience a selfobject breakdown and may react with anxiety and anger.

In his study comparing these groups to more traditional cognitive-behavioral approaches, Saunders found that abusive men diagnosed with more dependent personalities—as opposed to more antisocial personalities—were more successful with the process/psychodynamic approach. He found that the men were more engaged in this process and that many respond better to the more "compassionate" approach.

The Compassion Workshop

Stosny (1995) has designed a treatment program called The Compassion Workshop, which is based on the idea that most batterers cannot sustain attachment. Much like the approach advocated by Harway and Evans (1996) with the Cycle of Feeling Avoidance, this approach emphasizes the deficits in men's abilities to tolerate and regulate dysphoric affect. As Gottman (1994) has discovered, men easily become flooded and insist on either shutting down emotionally or lashing out at the perceived source of the pain when they experience narcissistic injuries. The Compassion Workshop employs a series of intense exercises, videos, and homework assignments to help the men generate increased compassion for the self: in other words, to repair deficits in the self-cohesion. The *HEALS* technique (the centerpiece of this program) teaches the men five steps towards awareness and reframing of dysphoric emotional states: Healing, Explain to Yourself, Apply Self-Compassion, Love Yourself, Solve. By practicing this technique frequently on a daily basis, the men are taught that compassion for the self and for others represents true power and has the ability to heal. Initial studies of The Compassion Workshop tentatively suggest lower dropout rates and lower post-treatment recidivism than with many other programs that have been similarly evaluated.

Solution-Focused Approaches

Solution-focused therapy (O'Hanlon & Weiner-Davis, 1989) emphasizes the strengths and potential of the individual rather than the problems and dysfunctions. It is a collaborative model that is influenced by a humanistic perspective, systems theory, and social constructivism. Proponents believe that lasting, positive changes can occur by focusing on current client strengths, competencies, and solution-building abilities rather than deficiencies. Language is viewed as the medium through which personal meanings are constructed. The language is one of "solution and strengths" rather than "deficits and blame." Clinicians assist clients with a series of questions that relentlessly reframe the person and the problem:

- (Exceptions) What is different about the times when you *don't* blow up?
- (Outcome) Suppose that one night, while you were asleep, there was a miracle and this problem was solved. How would you know? What would be different?
- (Coping) How exactly do you manage to cope with the stresses in your marriage and family?
- (Scaling) I know you are still losing your temper sometimes, but have you noticed how much lower in frequency (intensity, duration) these outbursts are?

Lee and colleagues (1997) designed a solution-focused brief group treatment for domestic violence offenders based on these principles. Without denying the aggressive or violent nature of the behaviors, group leaders were trained to avoid confronting clients and provoking defensiveness, to avoid getting into debates, and to take a "one-down" position and see the client as an "expert" on his situation. Group members engage in multiple homework assignments emphasizing identification of already-existing personal strengths and resources. The men in the programs are viewed as capable and willing to control their violence—by finding evidence through investigating past successes at avoiding abusive behavior. Rather than focusing on times of violence, the emphasis is on the exceptions to violence.

Countertransference Issues

In developing an empathic connection with men who have committed very disturbing and destructive acts, it is sometimes easy to fall prey to an overidentification with the perpetrator—and to forget that he is in treatment because someone else has been seriously hurt emotionally and/or physically. It can be difficult for clinicians to navigate the dual role of providing an empathic alliance and needing to report any signs of treatment failure or increased risk, and clinicians who cannot come to terms with this dual role should probably not treat this population. Unlike most other clinical treatment, the number one concern is the welfare of someone other than the client.

Nothing in this chapter should be construed as suggesting that this goal should be reduced or placed in the background—the arguments here have to do not with purpose, but with execution. When the clinician can maintain an empathic stance, he or she can relate to the batterer not as some disturbed social freak but rather as one more wounded man who has suffered narcissistic injuries and disappointments in his love relationship and at times finds this state unbearable—which leads to acting out at the perceived source of that frustration. Who among us does not know this experience?

Conclusion: Integration and Respect

From the philosophical and clinical perspective presented here, the treatment model that holds the most promise with the majority of this population is one that emphasizes the self psychological principles of client-centered respect, while not forsaking the psychoeducational information that these men need. This model is political, educational, and psychological. Some current treatment programs, such as DOMESTIC VIOLENCE 2000 and Foundations for Violence-Free Living (Amherst H. Wilder Foundation, 1995), integrate the psychoeducational format (teaching about the politics of abuse and cognitive-behavioral skills training) with these self psychological principles. While insisting that men take full responsibility for their abusive behavior, treatment approaches can still be most effective by addressing the psychological issues inherent in these destructive behaviors. Group leaders who can offer perpetrators a profound sense of respect for their experience—including their history, their experience of powerlessness, their emotional injuries in their primary relationships—are more likely to make an impact. We can lead men into new views of gender equality and new skills in self-management and communication best by first pacing their experience. By offering our respect, we model the ability for them to more fully respect themselves and others. By a compassionate understanding of their broken mirrors, we can help them develop new ways of finding twinship experiences with other men and even with their own female partners.

FEMINIST, COGNITIVE, AND BEHAVIORAL GROUP INTERVENTIONS FOR MEN WHO BATTER

An Overview of Rationale and Methods

Daniel G. Saunders, Ph.D.

This chapter is intended to give you a brief overview of feminist and cognitive-behavioral principles and techniques commonly used in working with men who batter. I begin with the rationale for using men's groups rather than couples therapy or mixed gender groups and end with a description of recent trends in interventions for men who batter.

Reasons to Focus on Men's Aggression in All-Male Groups

On the surface, it may appear that both men and women could benefit from a curriculum aimed at learning alternatives to aggression. Although some of the specific techniques of anger management can benefit both genders, the underlying causes of anger and aggression usually differ in men and women. For example, in cases of homicide, men's motives typically involve jealousy and possessiveness while women's involve self-defense (Saunders & Browne, in press). Men's aggression also remains the focus of most intervention programs because it is more destructive than women's aggression, both physically and psychologically (Straus & Gelles, 1990).

Even women who are arrested for assault cannot be assumed to have an "anger management" problem because the police and prosecutors may not have determined the "primary aggressor." Women who are violent are likely to have been victimized (Hamberger & Potente, 1994; Saunders & Browne, in press). Once they are free of violent relationships, they are less likely to use violence (Walker, 1984). Whereas men are generally conditioned to turn their hurt and fear into anger, anger may be less socially acceptable for women and they may use less direct ways to express it. Women's social skill groups tend to focus on helping women overcome nonassertiveness or passive-aggressiveness by expressing anger more directly. Men's anger, on the other hand, commonly arises from real or perceived threats to their power and fear

Portions of this chapter were condensed with permission from Saunders, D. (1989). Cognitive and behavioral interventions with men who batter: Application and outcome. In P. L. Caesar & L. K. Hamberger (Eds.), *Treating men who batter: Theory and practice.* New York: Springer

of abandonment (Dutton & Golant, 1995). Men who batter seem to have a better chance of changing aggressive patterns if they can explore male gender-role conditioning in an all-male group.

The majority of men's programs in North America combine ingredients from three major models of treatment: feminist, cognitive, and behavioral (e.g., Edleson & Tolman, 1992; Saunders, 1996a; Stordeur & Stille, 1989). Many of these programs also emphasize the benefits of the social support found in group treatment. There are additional reasons for a group format: confrontation of sexist and abusive beliefs is probably more effective from other group members and role-playing can be made more realistic. These groups rarely focus on building awareness of the childhood roots of aggression and helping to resolve childhood trauma, because it is assumed that this awareness will supply the men with more excuses for violence. Some models with this focus have recently been introduced (Browne, Saunders, & Staecker, 1997; Stosny, 1995).

A couples approach is usually not used in these programs because: (a) the preponderance of evidence indicates that the men and not the women have interpersonal skill deficits and traumatic childhoods, suggesting the need for long-term treatment (Hotaling & Sugarman, 1986); (b) women may not feel free to express their wishes and feelings when the men are present; (c) the women may be implicitly held co-responsible for the abuse merely by their presence in conjoint sessions (for a fuller discussion see Tolman & Edleson, 1995; Saunders, 1996a). Most men's group programs contend that a conjoint couples approach should be reserved for those cases in which the partners want to remain together, they are motivated to work on the relationship, and the man has completed enough treatment to control his violence. The advantages and disadvantages of a couples approach continue to be hotly debated in the field, and some states have developed standards to severely restrict or ban its use. Some research studies show promising results from couples group approaches, but these studies have usually screened out the most severe cases and used very small samples.

Feminist, Cognitive, and Behavioral Approaches

Feminist approaches are based on the assumption, and much evidence, that men's targets of aggression are often women and children even when the source of their anger is elsewhere. Aggression against women is seen as an attempt to maintain or regain male dominance in a society that views such dominance as the norm. Methods used in this approach are often didactic, but programs also use "control" logs, discussion, and confrontation. This approach is often integrated with cognitive restructuring, for example, by helping the men see the benefits for them of women's competence and independence.

Cognitive approaches are based on the assumption that anger is often a precursor of aggression and that cognitive distortions and irrational thoughts contribute to anger arousal. The stress inoculation therapy of Meichenbaum (1977) and Ellis' Rational Emotive Therapy are the primary cognitive approaches. The methods often use lectures, homework regarding personal events, and cognitive rehearsal.

Those using a cognitive framework assume that men's sense of entitlement and need for dominance are based on beliefs that are amenable to change. An approach based on inner conflicts between attitudes and core values has been used to confront abusive beliefs and male dominance (Russell & Frohberg, 1995).

Behavioral approaches are based on the assumption that men's aggression arises from a deficit in interpersonal skills or that they are hypersensitive to certain events. There is evidence, for example, that men who batter have a deficit of assertive skills

(Holtzworth-Munroe, 1992). Modeling and behavioral rehearsal are used to teach responsible assertive behavior. Systematic desensitization is used to overcome hypersensitivity to stressful and anger-arousing situations (Saunders, 1984; Stordeur & Stille, 1989).

There is no single theory or integrated set of procedures that can be called "cognitive-behavioral." Rather, the term covers a number of principles and procedures that many practitioners have not attempted to link theoretically. Cognitive and behavioral treatments have their roots in the principles and procedures of operant and classical conditioning. Bandura's (1973) social learning theory emphasized the cognitive aspects of these two conditioning principles and demonstrated in addition that much behavior is learned through imitation, without being conditioned. Modern social learning theory highlights the reciprocal influence of people and their environment and stresses the human capacity for self-directed change. O'Leary (1988) applies a social learning model to factors associated with wife abuse and finds that many factors fit the model well—for example, daily stressors and violence in the family of origin, combined with an aggressive personality style.

Cognitive and behavioral approaches, especially assertiveness training and relaxation training, have been quite popular in working with men who batter. National surveys of abuser programs show that the use of these procedures is widespread in all types of settings, including shelter-based and specialized programs, as well as more traditional service agencies (eg., Eddy & Myers, 1984). Other popular methods that are usually combined with cognitive-behavioral methods include the building of emotional awareness, sex-role resocialization, and the development of social support. One study showed that all of these methods can be integrated into a feminist-cognitive-behavioral approach (Saunders, 1996b). Even though programs may label themselves as "feminist" or "cognitive-behavioral," in reality they blend different approaches, with varying degrees of emphasis.

Although the above theories are typically applied in individual or group therapy, they can be adapted well to an educational format. I will expand on each approach below.

Application of Cognitive and Behavioral Principles

The description of cognitive and behavioral applications will be presented in the context of general principles that have been developed, tested, and applied for the alleviation of many types of problems. The application of cognitive-behavioral methods in working with men who batter usually consists of a combination of methods, most commonly assertiveness training, relaxation training, and some of the cognitive therapies (e.g., Edleson & Tolman, 1992; Ganley, 1981; Saunders, 1984; Sonkin & Durphy, 1989; Stordeur & Stille, 1989).

CONTINGENCY MANAGEMENT

The application of operant principles is called contingency management, because the immediate consequences, or contingencies, of behavior are modified. Aggression, like alcohol abuse, is a difficult behavior to treat because the abuser's discomfort and pain from the behavior are often delayed for a considerable period of time. The rewards, on the other hand, may be immediate, including, "having one's way" or a reduced fear of abandonment if the partner threatens to leave and then stays. The analysis of rewards and punishments fits the exchange/social control model.

Men entering abuser programs are often motivated to attend the programs out of a fear of punishment—either the formal punishment of criminal justice sanctions or the loss of their partners. Fear of punishment may also have an impact on the abusive behavior itself. When women tell their partners they will not return to them until they enter or complete treatment, they are applying negative reinforcement, i.e., his pain will end when he complies with her request. There is evidence that arrest, fear of arrest, and warnings of legal action are deterrents for some types of abusers (Saunders, 1994). There is also evidence, however, that arrest alone is not enough and that arrest plus treatment is much more effective (Saunders, 1996a).

Steinfeld (1986) gives examples of questions that therapists can ask abusers to make them more aware of the potential rewards and costs for aggression:

A. Gain via the aggressive behavior: *"What, specifically, Joe, did you want to happen when you hit Mary?"* Responses might include such factors as:
   1. Remove aversive behavior—"She was nagging me"; "I wanted to get away."
   2. Vindictiveness—"I wanted to hurt her back."
   3. Power—"I felt so helpless with her"; "I wanted to get through to her, to make her hear me out"; "I wanted to beat her to a pulp."
   4. Control—"I should tell her what to do"; "I'm the boss."
   5. Ego enhancement—"If I let her do that, what kind of man would I be? I can't let her push me around."
B. Strength of punishment: *"What, specifically, did you feel might happen if you hit her?"* Responses might include:
   1. "Nothing."
   2. "She could hit me back, kill me. She could leave."
   3. "Cops would come—things would blow over."
   4. "I could go to jail."
   5. "I would be fined."
C. Probability of payoff: *"What is the likelihood that the above (punishment, response costs) would actually occur?"*

Since research suggests that the consequences for behavior are most powerful if they are immediate and certain, program counselors can work with the criminal justice system to create policies that consistently and quickly hold men accountable for violent behavior. This is most feasible when the men are on probation or parole, because under such conditions the system can respond quickly yet flexibly. These methods are likely to work best for premeditated, instrumental violence, because the offender must be able to weigh the response costs and see the deterrent effects of punishment. If offenders are intensely angry, their perceptions may be too clouded to permit assessment of their behavior. Although community-based treatment or jail may seem like the only options, Tolman (1996) describes a range of sanctions that can be considered. Working with the criminal justice system and other agencies to formulate a coordinated community response to battering may appear to go beyond the role of "therapy," unless therapy is defined broadly as part of a social response to a social problem (Fagan, 1996).

A component of behavioral treatment of men who batter that has an element of extinction (the removal of positive reinforcement for the problem behavior) is the "time-out technique" (Sonkin & Durphy, 1989). With time-out, the abuser recognizes the build-up of anger, tells his partner he is taking a time-out, and then leaves for an hour or more in order to cool off. It is meant to be a time-out from conflict and angry emotions, but it may also operate as an extinction technique because the abuser does not get his way. This method is not appropriate for men who consistently use it to angrily reject their partners or find other ways to manipulate the technique in abusive ways.

The shame, guilt, and anxiety that some men feel following their aggression, from either external or internal sources, are probably short-lived means of behavior change. Indeed, for the type of man who already feels excessive guilt, more punishment may increase aggressiveness. Behavior therapists recommend that any punishment be quickly followed by an offer to teach the person positive behavior.

Positive reinforcement is used most commonly in treating men who batter by giving praise for learning skills that are incompatible with aggression. Naturally, this reinforcement is most powerful if a positive relationship has been formed with the client. Such a relationship can be built through an understanding of the client's feelings and acceptance of his humanity. In a group setting, the men can be taught to praise each other by making specific, reinforcing comments for reports of progress during the week and for acquiring new skills. This peer support appears to be one of the strongest forms of reinforcement the men can receive, and they report that it is a very useful part of the group experience. Through such support the men can lessen the strong dependence for praise and acceptance they often have on their partners. The men's overdependence on others can be decreased even more if they learn to praise themselves, a skill stressed by some cognitive therapists.

Because many of the men have low self-esteem, it may be very difficult for them to accept praise or to think of ways in which they have made progress. One way to overcome this difficulty is to begin group sessions with each man stating one way in which he applied a skill used in the group. When a man says "nothing" as his response, it may take several prompts to encourage him to relate a success. In later sessions, the men are taught to give specific, positive feedback to each other as they acquire skills.

AROUSAL REDUCTION

Although anger is neither a necessary nor sufficient condition for woman abuse or other forms of aggression, it is often associated with it. One of the necessary ingredients of anger and other emotions, however, is physiological arousal. Thus, if such arousal can be reduced, anger can be reduced as well. Behavior therapists have long used relaxation training, biofeedback, and similar methods to treat anxiety. These same methods are now being used to reduce the arousal component of anger and the stress reactions that occur before it (e.g., Deffenbacher, McNamara, Stark, & Sabadell, 1990).

The most common way to reduce physiological arousal is to teach "progressive relaxation." A large number of muscle groups are used at first, with the therapist instructing the client to alternately tense and release them. As the client gains experience, fewer muscle groups are used, with the client eventually being able to relax quickly by simply recalling the feelings of relaxation or by repeating a word that has been associated with the relaxed state. Because the training is usually conducted in a prone position with eyes closed, many men may resist practicing the exercises. This resistance may be especially pronounced in a group setting with other aggressive men. Some men feel more comfortable in a sitting position or turned away from the group.

As an adjunct or substitute for progressive relaxation, some men may find other relaxation methods more useful. There are a number of possible substitutes for relaxation that appeal to men, for example: biofeedback, because it is "high-tech," or Tai Chi, the martial art that is a form of exercise, relaxation, and meditation.

CLASSICAL CONDITIONING

Once relaxation is mastered, it can be combined with a series of anger-producing scenes, following the principles of classical conditioning (systematic desensitization) (Saunders, 1984). In the application of this method, we do not use the term "desensitization" but rather refer to the method as an "anger ladder." For homework, the client constructs a "ladder" of about three scenes, from the least to most upsetting. Following relaxation, the therapist alternates a calm scene with an anger-producing scene several times, until the stress or anger of the anger-producing scene is lessened or eliminated. It is important to begin with a scene very low in anger, otherwise the method will be ineffective. If a man reports no progress, he may need extra help constructing scenes low on the hierarchy. For example, instead of a scene of his boss yelling at him, he may find a less upsetting one, perhaps waiting for a train to pass on the way home from work.

COGNITIVE THERAPIES

Cognitive methods are among the most difficult to apply because the men are asked to look inward and focus on "irrational" or "automatic" thoughts. The methods are important, however, because they place responsibility for anger arousal clearly on the individual, not on the interaction. In contrast to social skills training, they also have the advantage of being applied to situations that are not interpersonal, for example, anger that might result from bad weather, lost keys, or being stuck in a traffic jam.

The most commonly used cognitive methods with men who batter are those which Novaco (1975, 1978) and others (e.g., McKay, Rogers, & McKay, 1989) adapted from the stress inoculation work of Meichenbaum (1977).

Novaco explains that aggression has several components. First, there are certain unmet expectations or faulty appraisals of aversive events. The subsequent arousal is labeled as anger, which may then lead to aggression. Clients are given the rationale that anger is often related to self-doubt or feelings of threat. They are taught to distinguish between self-defeating and self-enhancing statements that will help them to cope. If these are difficult to uncover, clients can be placed in a role-play situation until anger is aroused and then asked to "talk aloud" their anger-producing self-talk.

Clients are then taught to use self-statements at various stages of a situation that typically arouses anger. The situations are made more manageable by breaking them into stages: preparation, entering the situation, coping with arousal, and subsequent reflection. Novaco gives examples of each: "Remember, stick to the issue and don't take it personally" (preparation); "You don't need to prove yourself. Don't make more out of this than you have to" (impact); "Muscles are getting tight. Relax and slow things down" (arousal); "I handled that one pretty well. That's doing a good job" (conflict resolved); "Try to shake it off. Don't let it interfere with your job" (conflict unresolved). Such coping statements can be given to the men, but the exercise is likely to be more effective if the men shape their own statements. Often the statements are not very "believable" for the men. Relaxation applied with the statements may help the statements "sink in" and feel real. The men may also need help re-shaping some of the statements, trying out a number of statements suggested by the therapist until one is at least somewhat believable.

Other cognitive methods have also been applied, for example Ellis's (1977) Rational Emotive Therapy (RET) (Edleson & Tolman, 1992). RET helps clients confront irrational beliefs that lead to unrealistic expectations of themselves and others. The premise is that anger is likely to result if men believe they MUST always have the love and approval of those close to them. Anger may also be aroused if they believe that they must be thoroughly competent in all they do, or if they view life as catastrophic when things do not go the way that they want. Ellis gives numerous examples of ways to understand and dispute self-angering philosophies. He divides the analysis of self-statements into four categories. For instance, in response to a broken agreement:

- Rational belief: "What a bad action!"
- Irrational belief: "How AWFUL, I just can't stand her treating me in that manner. She SHOULD NOT, MUST NOT behave that way toward me, and I think that she is a HORRIBLE PERSON for doing so and that she SHOULD BE PUNISHED!"
- Appropriate consequence: disappointment, feelings of rejection.
- Inappropriate consequence: feelings of hostility and the desire for revenge or punishment.

Meichenbaum (1977) makes the point that the lack of coping techniques may be a bigger problem than the presence of irrational beliefs; thus cognitive and behavioral coping skills may be essential. Ellis also stresses the need to practice new behaviors outside of therapy. Closely related to RET is Beck's analysis of dysfunctional cognitive styles. These styles include the tendency to make arbitrary inferences, to magnify the meaning of an event, to use rigid, "black and white" thinking, and to overgeneralize (e.g., taking a single mistake as a sign of incompetence). Bedrosian (1982) shows how he helped a husband detect his automatic thoughts:

TH: What were you thinking when your wife came home?

H: I don't remember. It was just bullshit.

TH: Okay. Can you remember where you were and what you were thinking when you first realized she was late?

H: Well, I was sitting downstairs on the couch. The first thing I thought was, what if she had an accident?

TH: How did you feel then?

H: Scared. I remembered her accident from last month.

TH: So then what did you think when she came home?

H: First I was relieved. Then I thought, she's always doing this to me, she doesn't give a shit about me, all I do is work my tail off for this family, and this is the thanks I get.

TH: And then you hit the ceiling.

Bedrosian explains how the husband would experience fear when he thought about threats to his wife's safety and then disappointment when she did not call him. These feelings quickly turned to anger, however, because he interpreted her actions as personally directed at him.

Another cognitive therapy approach, called problem-solving treatment (D'Zurilla & Goldfried, 1971) has not been used directly with abusers. However, the mutual problem-solving and support that occur in many groups for men who batter use some steps of systematic problem-solving.

Cognitive methods are especially compatible with feminist approaches. They can be used to change the feelings of threat that some of the men feel from women's independence and competence. Cognitive restructuring can help turn typical male "scripts" of possessiveness, competition, and achievement-striving into more flexible behavior. For example, the self-statement "I must win every argument" can be transformed into the self-statement "If I win, we lose."

With the growing recognition that a substantial proportion of men who batter in treatment have a range of personality disorders, cognitive therapy for these disorders is being applied. The most common disorders seem to be narcissistic, passive-aggressive, and antisocial (Gondolf, 1999), but no single personality profile is apparant. Beck and Freeman (1990) describe cognitive conceptualizations, assessment strategies, and specific cognitive interventions for personality disorders. The assessment of personality disorders can help the counselor strike a balance between an overly rejecting stance and being manipulated. Understanding common counselor reactions to these clients is useful. For example, initial feelings of satisfaction often occur in response to clients with narcissistic features, since these clients are adept at using flattery. The feelings may soon give way to feelings of frustration at their lack of progress. Clients with antisocial personalities may produce frustration and hopelessness because of their resistance and slow progress. Reacting with anger may only feed into the "game plan" of these clients.

Another recent development in cognitive therapy is the recognition of "maladaptive schemas" that arise from childhood traumas. In particular, Young (1990) hypothesizes a link between schemas involving abandonment and mistrust and their expression in generalized beliefs, for example, beliefs that "I'll be alone forever. No one will be there for me," or "People will hurt me, attack me, take advantage of me. I must protect myself." These stable schemas and their expression seem to best characterize the subgroup abusers with borderline traits. There is evidence that they suffered severe emotional rejection in childhood and developed strong fears of abandonment as a result (Dutton & Holtzworth-Munroe, 1997).

MODELING AND REHEARSAL

Modeling and rehearsal have strong scientific support as a means of learning new behaviors. They are used to help the men acquire assertive and other social skills that are incompatible with aggression. Assertiveness is needed in situations where anger is justified but the man is typically passive—until he blows up. These social skills are also useful if the man is typically dominant and impulsive. Several studies indicate that men who batter are generally nonassertive, but there also appears to be a subtype of men who are generally dominant and aggressive both inside and outside of the home (Holtzworth-Munroe & Stuart, 1994). Assertiveness training is intended to teach the men to cope with criticism, make requests, say "no" assertively, empathize with others' feelings, and express feelings appropriately. The emphasis is on responsible assertiveness and egalitarian decision-making (Saunders, 1984). The group leader models each skill in a role-play and then guides each client through a role-play rehearsal using a "canned" situation. The skills can then be applied to real-life situations, which the men are asked to descibe specifically. They are helped to define a "critical moment" at which an assertive rather than passive or aggressive path could have been taken. After a skill is applied in a role-play rehearsal, the men receive constructive feedback from the leader and group members. The feedback focuses on non-verbal as well as verbal communication. The client then rehearses the situation again using the feedback. Often these situations do not involve the partner, but rather focus on a stressful problem at work, which is a major source of stress for many of the men. The steps of behavioral rehearsal are described in detail in a number of leader manuals (e.g., Lange & Jakubowski, 1976; Rose, 1989).

By the end of treatment, it should be possible to integrate most of the cognitive-behavioral skills that have been described above. For example, in rehearsing a new behavior, a client should be able to assess the costs and rewards of keeping aggressive behavior, identify and restructure cognitive distortions, relax away tension, and communicate assertively. It is hoped that the building blocks of skills that have been constructed throughout treatment can be combined quickly into a new habit.

Advantages and Disadvantages of These Methods

There are a number of advantages in the use of the methods just described. First, they are based on scientifically derived principles that have been used with other aggressive populations and so they can be evaluated more easily than most. For example, role-play assessments can be conducted inside or outside of a group setting with ratings of skill acquisition made by leaders and/or members. Second, because the methods are concrete and skill-based, clients often greet them with little resistance, they can be learned relatively quickly, and the methods can be transferred between programs. Third, the methods are quite compatible with feminist approaches and with the goals of the criminal justice system. The methods do not presume that the violence is the symptom of an underlying mental disorder or relationship problem; rather, the anger and violence are usually addressed directly. Finally, because the methods are based on the assumption that aggression is learned behavior over which self-control is possible, clients and practitioners may have more hope for change than if they were faced with instinctual or genetic theories of aggression.

Among the disadvantages, there is the risk that these methods will not be able to overcome the social reinforcement for woman abuse in our society if they are not integrated with a profeminist approach. As with some other approaches, cognitive-behavioral methods may seem like a "quick fix" to the men, their partners, and therapists, and false hopes may develop after short-term gains are made. However, the methods seem to offer the best hope for stopping the abuse quickly so that other methods can be used. Another disadvantage is that, if the partners are not well-informed about the training, the men's first attempts to communicate in new ways may bring negative comments from their partners, who see the behavior as phony. Finally, it has become clear that most of the men were traumatized as children, either by being abused or witnessing their mothers being abused. If violence in the nuclear family is from displaced aggression or unresolved anger from childhood, then cognitive-behavioral methods may be need to be supplemented with methods that resolve early trauma.

Feminist Approaches

Feminist approaches are "meta-methods" rather than a set of concrete procedures. They provide a lens through which we can critically examine our theories, methods, and behaviors as group leaders. They help us to answer the question: Is our thinking and relating consistent with the goal of gender equality? As with cognitive-behavioral approaches, feminist approaches cannot be easily subsumed under one type. They are often equated with educational methods that try to increase the men's awareness of the instrumental nature of their abuse (Pence & Paymar, 1993). This approach tends to confront men about the intentionality of their abuse and tries to make sure the men see the full range of abusive behaviors.

However, there are other approaches, like many of the cognitive-behavioral approaches covered above, that aim to increase the men's respect and equal treatment of women without confronting them about their dominant positions. One approach is to emphasize the toxic effects of men's constricted roles and then to build awareness of the benefits of expanded roles, including roles of housework and childcare, to reduce the burden on their partners. Many intervention guides for helping men who batter focus on changing men's gender-role socializations (Gondolf & Russell, 1987; Lindsey, McBride, & Platt, 1993; Stordeur & Stille, 1989). There are also more general descriptions of traditional male scripts and ways to change them (e.g., Kivel, 1992; Stoltenberg, 1993). Kivel and his associates at the Oakland Men's Project makes clear the connections that exist between sexism, racism, classism and homophobia—and they do so in a non-shaming way.

Even with a general consensus about the goal of gender equality, there is room for plenty of debate in the field. For example, some programs insist that male leaders be used and that male-female teams not be used out of fear that the men will think that abuse is a male-female "relationship problem." Other programs claim that male-female teams are advantageous because they model good communication and conflict resolution between the men and women. Similarly, there seems to be consensus in all these approaches around the need to point out the objectification of women when it occurs in group (for example, men are asked to use their partners' first names rather than referring to them as "the woman," "the wife," or something more derogatory). However, leaders differ on the appropriate timing for such confrontations. Some group leaders prefer to wait until after they have built rapport with the men before confronting the most blatant sexist remarks (Browne, Saunders, & Staecker, 1996).

Do We Know What Works?

The studies of treatment effectiveness conducted so far (reviewed in Saunders, 1996a; Tolman & Edleson, 1995) indicate some promise for using integrated feminist-cognitive-behavioral approaches for stopping or reducing assaults. Some studies also show promise for reducing levels of anger, depression, and rigid sex-role beliefs. The evidence is less encouraging for the reduction of psychological abuse. No firm conclusions can be made at this time about the efficacy of a cognitive-behavioral approach because of the many flaws in the studies' designs. For example, most studies do not try to control for factors such as separation of the couple or arrest of the abuser, which are likely to have a strong impact on the men's behavior.

There exists some evidence that different types of treatment may be needed for different types of offenders. For example, in an experimental comparison that I conducted of feminist-cognitive-behavioral and process-psychodynamic approaches, men with dependent personalities had significantly lower recidivism rates in an unstructured process-psychodynamic group than in a structured feminist-cognitive behavior group (Saunders, 1996b). A small sample study comparing men's groups with couples groups found no overall differences between the groups, but found a tendency for the couples group to be more effective if the husband abused alcohol (Brannen & Rubin, 1996).

Group leaders need to be alert to the latest scientific findings of intervention outcome research. Careful reading of the studies will indicate whether the studies used adequate sample sizes and women's reports of their partners' behavior many months after treatment. Studies are now reporting 80% follow-up interview rates with partners over a year after treatment, whereas earlier studies reported only 40–60% follow-up rates. Studies with random assignment to comparison or control groups are beginning to appear. As more rigorous research finds its way into the field, interventions will become more effective.

Recent Trends

There are several important trends in the field that are helping to refine and improve all of approaches described above.

First, research indicates an emerging profile of the most dangerous men. As a result, some programs carefully assess for levels of violence severity and then place the men into different intervention "tracks." The Third Path in Arapahoe County, Colorado, is one such program (Healy, Smith, & O'Sullivan, 1998). Intake workers need to keep in mind that risk factors for increased danger during the relationship may be different from risk factors during separation (Saunders & Browne, in press).

Second, a "transtheoretical" approach, called stages of change (Prochaska & DiClemente, 1992), is being applied to interventions with men who batter. The assumption is that the particular approach is less important than recognizing the man's level of motivation. A further assumption is that treatments are more effective when they are matched to the individual's level of motivation—from pre-contemplation, to contemplation of change, to preparation, to action, and finally to maintenance of change.

Third, progress is being made in deepening the cultural competence of programs (Carrillo & Tello, 1998). This is partly in response to findings that show a higher rate of program attrition for men of color. Williams and Becker (1994) describe several organizational avenues for developing cultural competence, including staff training, consultation, and self-evaluation. They also stress the need for outreach to communities of color. Some programs use same-race groups, and there are indications of increased cohesion in such groups (Williams, 1995). Some programs emphasize that confrontation may be culturally inappropriate. For example, Asian counselors at the EMERGE program in Boston developed a nonconfrontational socratic method that used metaphors and parables. They even avoided the term "batterer." Some programs make use of culturally specific rituals and concepts, for example, Native Americans' use of sweat lodges, the burning of sage, and the medicine wheel. Counselors need to ask a series of questions when assessing "resistance" of men of color. Has institutional racism led to poor education and employment opportunities? Does our program "push" men out of treatment due to the high educational level of our material? Do we understand and help men face daily racial hassles and daily survival needs?

Fourth, communities are increasingly developing a coordinated response to domestic violence that involves several key agencies. Several studies indicate that a combination of arrest, fines, and treatment is more effective than any one of these "ingredients" alone. Coordinating bodies and task forces provide several functions: congruent policies can give a consistent message to offenders; referral practices can be improved; and mutual consultation and cross-training reduce mistrust among different professionals and enhance everyone's skills. In addition, these agencies often join together on domestic violence prevention campaigns. In recent years, more health-care and child welfare workers have joined the effort.

Finally, more programs seem to be emphasizing social action as a phase of "treatment" and developing community-wide anti-violence initiatives. For example, near the end of treatment the men might be encouraged to organize a talk about domestic violence at a local high school. Some programs train reformed men to "sponsor" other men. Men leaving our programs can have a positive "ripple effect" on their friends, coworkers, and sons, and sometimes on the community at large. Only by involving a wider circle of men and boys can we be sure of decreasing violence in succeeding generations.

STANDARD FORMS

WEEKLY CHECK-IN

 **Handout**

Name: _____   Date: _____

1. **WEEKLY SUCCESS.** Describe one way in the past week in which you successfully kept yourself from being aggressive or successfully used something you learned in group. The success can be large or small. Give yourself permission here to "pat yourself on the back."

Specifically, did you do any of the following:

___ calmly stood up for my rights
___ expressed my feelings responsibly
___ told myself to relax
___ changed my thoughts from negative to positive
___ took a time-out

2. **PROBLEM SITUATION.** Describe a problem situation from the past week. What did you say or do specifically?

How upset did you become?

1	10	20	30	40	50	60	70	80	90	100

Not at   Extremely
All Upset   Upset

3. **AGGRESSION.** Did you become verbally or physically aggressive toward anyone in the past week (including threats and damage to property)?

Yes ___   No ___   If yes, what did you do?

___ slapping   ___ chocking
___ kicking   ___ sexual abuse
___ punching   ___ verbal abuse
___ throwing things   ___ other (explain) _____

What would you do in a similar situation in the future to avoid becoming aggressive?

4. Did you complete homework for the week?   Yes _____   No _____
   If yes, what did you do?   Read handouts?   Yes _____   No _____
                                     Completed written assignment?   Yes _____   No _____
                                     Practiced exercise?   Yes _____   No _____

Date: _____ Time: _____	**LEVEL OF GROUP PARTICIPATION**	
Group Name: _____	Participated Frequently: Disclosed	____
Group Therapists:	Participated Frequently: Offered Feedback	____
_____ / _____	Participated Moderately	____
Group Topic: _____	Participated Rarely, but Appeared Attentive	____
Session #: _____ Present ____	Participated Rarely, Appeared Fatigued or Preoccupied	____
Absent ____	Failure to Participate: Appeared Unmotivated	____
	Obstructive to Group Process	____
	Resistant to Information	____
	Appears to be Using Course Material	____
	Completed Homework	____

AFFECT
Upbeat _____
Guarded _____
Resentful _____
Calm _____
Frustrated _____
Reflective _____
Inappropriate _____
Flat _____
Angry _____
Sad _____
Anxious _____
Confident _____
Regretful _____
Other _____

COGNITIONS
Hopeful/Hopeless
1 2 3 4 5

Positive/Negative Self-Talk
1 2 3 4 5

Clear/Confused
1 2 3 4 5

Not evident from this session ____

Other _____

RESPONSIBILITY FOR SELF
Takes Responsibility/Little Taken
1 2 3 4 5

Blaming others _____

Helplessness _____

Not evident from this session _____

THERAPEUTIC CONCERNS
Incident of
   Re-abuse _____
Suicidality _____
Increased Risk _____
   of Re-abuse
Hostile, _____
   Aggressive
   Behavior
Increased _____
   Depression
Increased Stress _____
Other _____

CPS Report _____

Warning to Victim _____

Other _____

GROUP PROGRESS NOTE

Group Member's Name: _____

Comments: _____

_____

_____

Signature: _____

Date of Note: _____

EVALUATION FORM

Group Member's Name: _____

Group Therapists' Names: _____ / _____

Group Attended: _____ Dates: _____ to _____

Total # sessions attended: _____ Date of report: _____

Please evaluate the group member on all the scales listed below. The norm group should be the overall population of group members at this stage of treatment. Give a "1" for the lowest score on each item and a "9" for the highest score, with any number in between which best describes your assessment.

PARTICIPATION

Isolates self	1	2	3	4	5	6	7	8	9	Discloses frequently
Never initiates	1	2	3	4	5	6	7	8	9	Initiates frequently
Gives no feedback	1	2	3	4	5	6	7	8	9	Shares feedback frequently
Defensive	1	2	3	4	5	6	7	8	9	Very open to feedback
Feedback aggressive/destructive	1	2	3	4	5	6	7	8	9	Feedback constructive
Does not complete homework	1	2	3	4	5	6	7	8	9	Completes homework

BEHAVIOR

Poor ability to express feelings	1	2	3	4	5	6	7	8	9	Excellent ability to express variety of feelings
Does not recognize responsibility for family violence	1	2	3	4	5	6	7	8	9	Recognizes responsibility
Poor control over impulses and behavior	1	2	3	4	5	6	7	8	9	Good control
Minimal empathy/concern for victim or other family members	1	2	3	4	5	6	7	8	9	Excellent empathy/concern
Low self-esteem	1	2	3	4	5	6	7	8	9	Excellent self-esteem/self-respect
Little self-awareness of buildup of tension or emotional needs	1	2	3	4	5	6	7	8	9	Excellent self-awareness
Frequent use of "controlling" behavior	1	2	3	4	5	6	7	8	9	Excellent tolerance for behavior of others
Poor assertive expression	1	2	3	4	5	6	7	8	9	Excellent assertiveness of needs and feelings

Please rate the group member's overall progress, as compared to the overall population of group members at this stage of treatment. Rate on a scale of 1–9, with 1 as no improvement and 9 as outstanding improvement.

        1   2   3   4   5   6   7   8   9   N/A

At this time, check the box if you recommend either of the following:

Probation ____

Termination from program ____

COMMENTS

_____

_____

_____

_____

_____

_____

Group cotherapist signature _____

Group cotherapist signature _____

MEN'S GROUP ORIENTATION

 **Handout**

Welcome to the group counseling sessions offered for the treatment of domestic violence. The following is a list of answers to frequently asked questions about the groups. **Please read this information carefully.**

1. *Why were you referred for domestic violence treatment?*

   You were referred to this program because of a report that indicated that you were involved in an incident of family violence. The fact that you have been referred to a Men's Group indicates that these problems are treatable.

2. *How often do the groups meet?*

   Each group meets for two hours, once a week for 32 weeks.

3. *What happens in the group?*

   Each session is designed to focus on a particular aspect of family violence. Groups offer a chance for men to discuss family problems, feelings that have led to destructive behavior, and the impact violence has had on the relationship. We strongly emphasize new ways of communicating, handling stress, and resolving conflicts.

4. *Is this a class or group counseling?*

   Although many of the group sessions involve teaching specific skills such as stress management and improved communication, the groups are considered to be "group counseling." This means that we encourage group members to think about their own lives, discuss feelings, and offer support for other group members. Men benefit from the group based on how fully they get involved.

5. *Do I have to come every week?*

   Group members are required to attend. Research indicates that there is a direct relationship between steady attendance and treatment progress. In order for you to benefit from the program, attendance must become a priority. As you become more involved in the group, you will probably find that you are motivated to attend, not only for your own benefit, but also to support your fellow group members.

6. *What about absences?*

   Documentation of all excused absences is required and should be given to the group counselors prior to your absence. Undocumented absences will be considered unexcused. Unexcused absences (those not as a result of documented illness or other emergency) indicate a lack of interest or commitment to change your situation. One unexcused absence will result in a review of your case. Any additional unexcused absences may result in your termination from the program. Three excused absences are the maximum allowed during your participation in this program, with only one allowed during the first eight weeks.

7. *What happens if I arrive late?*

   If a group member arrives more than ten minutes late, he will be considered as absent and will not receive credit for that session.

8. *Who leads the groups?*

   All of the group counselors are licensed clinical social workers, licensed clinical psychologists, or interns in psychology, social work, or marriage and family counseling who have had extensive training in treatment of domestic violence. Each group is co-led by a female and a male counselor.

9. *Are there additional expectations for successful participation other than group attendance?*

Most sessions have homework assignments that you will be expected to complete and bring to the next group meeting. The counselors will review the homework assignment with you at the end of each group meeting so you will know what is expected. The counselors will also discuss the completed homework at the beginning of each group meeting. Failure to complete the homework may result in your case being reviewed for possible termination from treatment services.

You will be given *DV 2000 Resources for Men* at your first group meeting. Each week, information from the resources will be discussed during the group session. You are expected to bring your notebook to each group meeting.

10. *What about confidentiality? Can what I say in the group be used against me?*

Since this treatment uses a team approach among counselors, you can assume that what you say in the group may be discussed with other counselors involved in your treatment and/or your probation officer (if applicable). Only information that directly relates to your treatment goals is included in these reports. Most of the personal issues and feelings discussed in the group sessions remain confidential.

In certain situations, the group counselors are obligated to report information that is revealed in the group. These reportable situations include serious threats of hurting or killing someone else, serious threats of hurting or killing yourself, and new and significant reports of child abuse.

ADDITIONAL INFORMATION AND RULES

1. Groups begin at the designated time. Group members are required to arrive ten minutes before the group start time to fill out a questionnaire entitled "Weekly Check-in." Group will not begin until everyone completes the questionnaire. Failure to complete the questionnaire will result in an unexcused absence.

2. No use of alcohol the day of group.

3. All program fees must be paid in full in advance of each group session or the group member will not be allowed to attend.

4. Group members will not threaten nor intimidate any group members or counselors at any time. Counselors and clients will ensure the safety of all group members.

5. The group counselors will evaluate your progress on a regular basis.

I have read the above information and agree to the conditions of treatment.

_____   _____
Group Member's Signature   Print Name

_____   _____
Date   Group Name

BRIEF
INTERVENTIONS

Session 1
HOUSE OF ABUSE

Materials:

Men's Group Orientation
"House of Abuse"
"Emotional Abuse & Mind Games"

Goal:

To introduce group members to the basic definitions of abuse and the range of intimidating behaviors.

Tasks:

1. *Introduce group leaders and group members.*
2. *Review Men's Group Orientation.*
3. *Ask each group member to sign contract.*
4. *Conduct group introduction exercise.*
5. *Explain "House of Abuse."*
6. *Identify different "rooms" of the House.*
7. *Review "Emotional Abuse & Mind Games."*
8. *Explain use of Weekly Check-in.*

Program:

1. Group leaders should introduce themselves.

2. Review the Men's Group Orientation. You do not have to read all sections aloud, but you should highlight most of them. Clarify the policies about homework, attendance, and confidentiality. Ask all group members to sign one copy of this contract and turn it in to you.

3. It is usually best to keep personal abuse and violence information to a minimum in the first session. Conduct a brief group introduction exercise with the following instructions: *Please pair up with one of the group members next to you. You will have a few minutes each to get some basic information from your "partner": What is*

43

his name? Is he currently married or together with his partner? What is her name? Does he have kids? What are their names and ages? Where is he from? What kind of work does he do? What are his interests and hobbies? You don't need to find out any details about how he ended up here in the group. We'll save that for much later. Then you will introduce your "partner" to the group. At the end of this, and throughout the early group sessions, group leaders should seek out ways to establish connections among group members, such as those who are parents, those who are from similar parts of the country, etc.

4. Begin explaining the basic concept of the House of Abuse by drawing a diagram of the House of Abuse on the board. By the end of this program, the following categories will be listed in the different rooms:

Physical	Verbal/Emotional/Psychological
Social Isolation	Male Privilege
Intimidation	Religion
Sexual	Child Abuse

As you go through this discussion, these questions should be asked repeatedly:

> Is this a house that you would like to live in?
>
> You don't have to say anything out loud, but see if you recognize any of these rooms as rooms in your house right now.
>
> Again, don't say anything out loud, but see if you recognize any of these rooms as rooms in the house you grew up in.

It is also important to repeatedly emphasize the "100% rule." This rule states that we are each 100% responsible for our own behavior. Being angry or hurt does not have to lead to abuse or intimidation. It has proven very valuable in this exercise to develop descriptions that are as gender-neutral as possible. Most of these forms of abuse can just as easily be used by a woman to a man as the other way around, with the obvious exceptions of male privilege, and, for the most part, sexual abuse. The goal here is to open up valuable discussion and to help the group members discuss these issues without feeling defensive.

Begin by asking for a definition of the most obvious kinds of abuse—this will usually involve physical abuse and probably yelling and screaming. Ask the question: *What are some ways that someone in an intimate adult relationship could be abusive to his or her partner? How can somebody abuse another?* As the group identifies different themes, label the different rooms and fill in some of the examples in the room where they best fit. Here are some basic descriptions of what belongs in each room:

a. **Physical.** This is the easiest to identify. This includes any kind of physical aggressive contact, including hitting, choking, pushing, etc. Make sure to review every possible form that the group can generate. The group members usually describe this first.

b. **Verbal/Emotional/Psychological.** This is also easy to identify. This includes any kind of name-calling, verbal put-downs, criticism, etc. This also involves the use of mind games. When a man "teases" a woman about her weight or body and then protests that he was only kidding or only asking a question, he is committing psychological abuse. When she humiliates him in public, she is doing the same thing. Often, men drill home the message that "you could never make it without me." When people hear this enough times, they may begin to believe it. Humiliating someone for not being successful or competent at something is psychological abuse. Another form of abuse in this category is ignoring someone: the silent treatment. This can be one of the most powerful mind games of all, wearing someone down until they desperately try to "be good."

c. **Intimidation**. This includes threats to kill or hurt the other person, threats against the kids, or threats of kidnapping the kids. It may involve telling her that a judge will never give her custody because she's crazy or she doesn't work or she has used drugs in the past. Threatening suicide is another example of intimidation—this can be a very powerful way of controlling someone because they are desperate to avoid the terrible guilt and pain. The goal of these gambits is to produce FEAR, which is used to maintain dominance and control.

d. **Sexual.** The most blatant form of sexual abuse is rape, which has only recently been declared a crime in a marriage. However, this is not the only form of sexual abuse in a relationship. Demanding that the partner watch or read pornography can be abusive. Insisting on certain sex acts that she finds humiliating or degrading can be abusive.

e. **Social Isolation.** This category is often overlooked. Because they feel threatened, men may become determined to prevent their wife or partner from becoming independent or successful. This may involve sabotaging the woman's attempts to work, go to school, or have friends or activities of her own. The fear for a man here is that the woman won't need him anymore if she develops in this way. This is the ultimate indication of insecurity— the man has to keep her down so that he can feel more confident and dominant.

f. **Male Privilege.** The male privilege form of abuse includes the entitlement men claim that leads them to dominate the relationship. The man who insists on using the fact that he is the breadwinner to demand that he make decisions for the marriage and family would be an example. This same attitude can be used to demand sex, get out of household chores, or demand more control over his free time than his wife or partner is allowed. A man may tell his wife or partner that he "needs" to go away with his buddies for a week; what would it be like if she told him the same thing, and if she just assumed that he would watch the kids and take care of the business at home?

g. **Religion**. Using religion as a form of abuse involves invoking the Bible as a rationalization for domination. It should be pointed out that, like statistics, the Bible can be interpreted as an explanation for just about anything. Be careful here—making remarks that might seem disrespectful about the Bible or religion can be very damaging to initial rapport. It is often helpful to start out by suggesting that one form of abuse can be restricting a partner's right to go to the church he or she wants or insisting that he participate in religion when he doesn't want to. As the discussion moves on, try asking the question, "How could someone use the Bible as a form of abuse?"

h. **Child Abuse**. Any physical, sexual, verbal, or emotional form of child abuse is likewise an abuse to the marriage. Using the kids as pawns in the battle between parents or threatening to hurt the kids would be examples here also. This can often lead to a discussion about the ways in which abused children often become abusers themselves in the next generation.

i. **The Roof.** This is the symbol of dominance and control. The theme to emphasize, eventually, is that this roof is supported by all the different rooms of the house. Even if the acts of abuse are not intended for this purpose, they all support dominance and control.

5. Introduce one more concept: the foundation. Feelings are in the foundation of the house, and when feelings are expressed in a non-abusive fashion, they strengthen this foundation. Ask the men to imagine what it would take to "clean" the House of Abuse? What would the house look like after the cleaning? And who is responsible for cleaning it?

6. Review "Emotional Abuse & Mind Games."

7. Explain how to fill out the Weekly Check-in each week.

The House of Abuse*

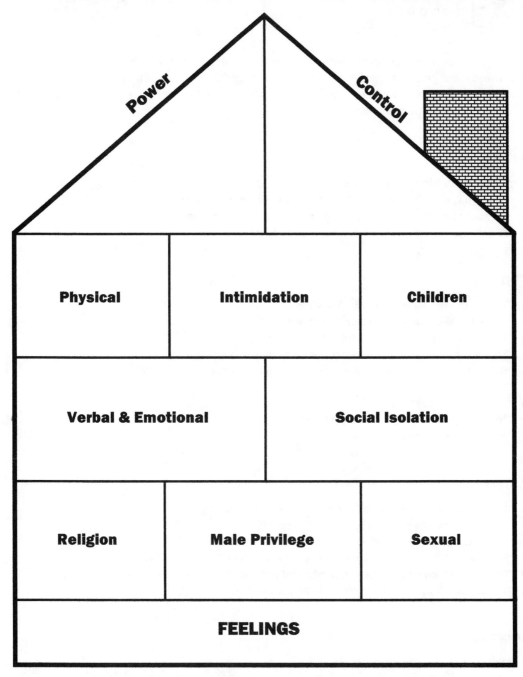

* The House of Abuse chart was developed by Michael F. McGrane, MSW, LICSW, Director of the Community Assistance Program (CAP) of the Amherst H. Wilder Foundation, and is used here by permission. The chart is part of a complete domestic abuse curriculum entitled Foundations for Violence-Free Living: A Step-by-Step Guide to Facilitating Men's Domestic Abuse Groups, available from the Wilder Publishing Center at 1-800-274-6024.

EMOTIONAL ABUSE & MIND GAMES

Handout

Like hitting, repeated emotional abuses can have severe effects on the victim's sense of self and of reality. These mind games sometimes leave more lasting damage than physical abuse. The person on the receiving end—male or female—may question his or her reality, feel powerless, become overdependent, etc. Here are some examples:

COERCION

- "I am going to kill myself if you leave me!"
- "Either you put out for me or I'm going to go find someone who will!"
- "I'm gonna take these kids right now and you'll never see them again!"
- "I'll get a doctor to say you're crazy and put you away!"

PUT-DOWNS

- "You're just like your mother: a fat, brainless ass!"
- "You're just like your father: a lazy, bull-headed ass!"
- "My wife can't cook for shit." (in front of other people)
- "My mother was right about you—you'll never amount to anything!"
- "How come a big, strong guy like you can't make more money around here?"
- "You're stupid."
- "You're acting crazy."
- "There you go again—crying like a big baby."
- "Nobody's ever going to want you!"

ISOLATION

- "I want to know everywhere you've been in the last 24 hours!"
- "I want to know where every penny has been spent!"
- "I know you go to that school just so you can try to pick up some girl!"
- "Your family just messes you up—I don't ever want you to talk to them again!"
- "No, you can't have the car. I might need it and you don't need to go anywhere."
- "You can't go out. I want you to stay right at home with me."

BLAMING

- "It's your fault my career is going nowhere."
- "Nobody else has ever made me violent! You must be doing something to cause this!"

MALE PRIVILEGE & CONTROL

- "You don't even know how to take care of yourself without me around!"
- "You have not cleaned up this house properly!"
- "I'll decide how the money gets spent!"
- "No wife of mine is going out to work—that's my job!"
- "I don't care what you think about my gambling habit—it's my money and I'll do what I want!"
- "So what if I bought that car without discussing it with you?"

SESSION 2
TIME-OUT

Materials:

> *Weekly Check-in*
> *"The Nine Commandments"*
> *"Time-out"*
> *"Time-out Information for Partners"*
> *"When Your Partner Blocks Your Path"*
> *"The Responsibility Plan"*

Goal:

> For each group member to develop a very specific plan for dealing with stressful family situations so that aggression can be minimized or avoided.

Tasks:

> 1. *Review Weekly Check-in.*
> 2. *Review "The Nine Commandments."*
> 3. *Explain "Time-out."*
> 4. *Review "Time-out Information for Partners."*
> 5. *Review "When Your Partner Blocks Your Path."*
> 6. *Review early warning signs for anger and escalation.*
> 7. *Review each step of "Responsibility Plan."*
> 8. *Guide all members in developing a Responsibility Plan.*
> 9. *Assign homework.*

Program:

> 1. Review "The Nine Commandments." Identify these as central themes that will be revisited time and again throughout the program. On #2, remember to identify several possible exceptions, such as self-defense or military action. On #8, be prepared for all group members to agree—even though you may discover later that they actually have many "attitudes" about the different rights or capabilities of men and women. To help destigmatize the group members, group leaders should

50

include personal examples in discussions about relationship problems, such as in the review of The Nine Commandments.

2. Introduce the idea of having a plan for episodes when it feels like behavior is getting out of control. This requires personal responsibility—to recognize the signals and to act responsibly in those situations. The odds of being successful with this plan are much higher when people have thought about it, planned for it, and rehearsed it in advance.

3. Review "Time-out": Aggression can be averted if the men can recognize the early warning signs of anger, non-aggressively say they need to leave for a while, and then take a time-out. The technique does not help the couple resolve the issue at hand; thus, it is a stopgap measure. However, it often prevents violence, which is the primary goal. Communication skills can be learned later, after the fear of violence is gone.

   Model the use of the skill with a co-leader or one of the men. If possible, have each man practice time-out, with some brief feedback given to him after each rehearsal. During the rehearsal, have the men actually walk away from the situation and quickly walk around the room.

   Make sure that the men inform their partners—*in advance*—of the purpose and steps involved with the time-out.

Ask these questions:

   ■ *Could you feel the anger being worked off when you were walking around?*
   ■ *What problems do you think you will have in using the technique?*

4. Review "Time-out Information for Partners." Be prepared for the group discussion in which the men protest that their partners will never put up with a time-out. It is important to empathize with this concern, because in many cases it is legitimate. Emphasize that we are offering approaches that are not guaranteed to work, but that do decrease the probability of an explosion.

5. Review "When Your Partner Blocks Your Path." One of the group members (or group leaders) should stand near the doorway, blocking the male's path out of the room. Explain to the men that their job, if ever blocked from being able to exit by their wife or partner in an explosive situation, is to find a way out without "putting hands on." This is a very controversial subject. The men in the group will often loudly complain—in some cases, rightfully so—that they don't have any good options in this situation. Our job here is to empathize with the difficulty of being in this position while strategizing the least dangerous and destructive ways to get out of it. It is essential to remind the men that all of these strategies contain significant risks, but that the alternative—violence between intimate partners—is worse.

6. Review anger's early warning signs in group discussion.

   Having some early warning signs of anger is like knowing how to read the sky to know if a storm is coming. We can learn the early warning signs of our anger by paying attention to physical cues inside of us—and then we can get away from the storm! The relaxation training will make it easier to recognize these signs. Simply being aware of the physical cues can help us to take action to stop the escalation of anger into aggression.

When we feel threatened we have a tendency to respond by fighting or fleeing. There is a powerful physiological response that is triggered.

Ask for physical cues that they notice in themselves and list them on the board. Common cues are: raised voice, pacing the floor, hot rush to the head, tightening arm muscles, rapid heartbeat.

7. Explain the different categories listed on the "Responsibility Plan." These categories are explained clearly on the handout. In the group, discuss different examples that may fit into each of the categories so that everyone gets the idea.

8. Ask group members to develop their own "Responsibility Plan." Each man should write it on his own form.

9. Present each "Responsibility Plan" to the group and review.

Homework

1. Explain what you have learned about time-out to your wife or partner, and rehearse how you will use this if necessary. **It is very important to make it clear that this is a sign of respect for the relationship, not an act of aggression or avoidance.**

2. Show your wife or partner the handout on "Time-out Information for Partners." Ask her to read it and sign to indicate that she understands the ideas. If she is unwilling to do so, **do not pressure her.** We will discuss this in the next group session.

3. After reviewing this information together, try using time-out two times during the week. If there is no situation that calls for it, imagine that there is one and rehearse your response together. Record below the words you used and actions you took. If you and your wife or partner are separated, describe two examples of how you would have used it in the past.

THE NINE COMMANDMENTS

Handout

1. We are all 100% responsible for our own behavior.

2. Violence is not an acceptable solution to problems.

3. We do not have control over any other person, but we do have control over ourselves.

4. When communicating with someone else, we need to express our feelings directly rather than blaming or threatening.

5. Increased awareness of self-talk, physical cues, and emotions is essential for progress and improvement.

6. We can always take a time-out before reacting.

7. We can't do anything about the past, but we can change the future.

8. Although there are differences between men and women, our needs and rights are fundamentally alike.

9. Counselors and case managers cannot make people change—they can only set the stage for change to occur.

TIME-OUT

 **Handout**

The time-out is an emergency strategy to prevent dangerous escalation of conflicts. It should <u>only</u> be used in crisis—and as you learn better communication and self-management skills, it may never have to be used at all. But you must know how to use it effectively.

Time-out should not be used as a weapon against the other person. It should not be used as a way of avoiding conflicts. It should not be used as a way of making the other person feel abandoned (*"I'm outta here, babe—I'll show you who's in charge!"*).

Instead, time-out should be used as a sign of respect for the relationship. The message is this: *"I care enough about us that I don't want any more damage to this relationship."*

It is essential that your wife or partner understand this message of respect. It is your job to clearly explain this to her, in advance—and to follow it up by your actions when using the time-out correctly.

1. *"I'm beginning to feel like things are getting out of control."*

2. *"And I don't want to do anything that would mess up our relationship."*

3. *"So I need to take a time-out."*

4. *"I'm going out for a walk around the neighborhood (or my sister's house, or the gym, etc.)."*

5. *"I'll be back in (five minutes, or one hour, etc.)."*

6. *"And let's try talking about this again when I get back. OK?"*

Partner responds:

7. *"OK. Time-out."*

If she does not acknowledge, begin the time-out anyway—<u>without</u> making any physical contact or threats!

- Leave silently—no door slamming.
- While away, don't drink or use drugs—and don't drive if your temper is out of control.
- Try using "self-talk" that will help you keep this in perspective:
  - *"I'm getting upset, but I don't have to lose my cool!"*
  - *"I'm frustrated, but I don't have to control anybody else or always get my way."*
  - *"I can calm myself and think through this situation."*
  - *"I've got to think about what will be most important for the future."*
- Do something physical (walking, playing sports, working out, etc.) if it will help you discharge tension. Try distracting yourself with any activity that temporarily takes your mind off the intensity of the argument.
- **You must come back when you said you would, or call and check in.** When you come back, decide together if you want to continue the discussion. Here are the options at this point:
  - **Discuss it now:** This is usually the best and most respectful action, but there are some exceptions.
  - **Drop the issue:** Maybe you both realize now that it was really not that big a deal.
  - **Put the issue on hold:** This may be important to discuss, but it would be better to do it at later time. As long as <u>both</u> parties agree, this can work.
- Each person has the right to say "no" to further discussion at that time and to suggest a time for discussion. If anger escalates again, take another time-out.

TIME-OUT INFORMATION FOR PARTNERS*

 **Handout**

1. How do time-outs help solve our family problems?

Your partner's use of time-outs will prevent him from escalating into physical or psychological abuse. Time-outs alone do not solve conflicts, but if used faithfully they will help him avoid using physical battering and some of the other tactics of control. Stopping the battering is the first step to resolving family problems. Family problems have to be discussed and solutions agreed upon. This cannot happen if one person is battering the other. No communication takes place when there is abuse. Time-outs are a necessary first step to communicating respectfully.

2. What do I do if every time I want to discuss an important topic with my partner, he says he is taking a time-out?

Let him take the time-out anyway. If he becomes angry and abusive, you will not be able to talk about the problems. At first he may take time-outs a lot. Just remind yourself that it is only one step and that he will be expected to use other approaches as well. Read the instruction sheet—it will help you understand how it works.

3. What if he refuses to discuss the matter even after the time-out?

Notice on the instruction sheet that he has several choices as to what he does after a time-out. He is not supposed to drop issues if they are important to you. However, he may put them on hold until he is able to both calmly speak and *listen to you*. If he refuses to discuss an issue, your insisting will *not* bring about the communication. Let him know that you are still interested in talking about the issue, but be willing to set a later time when he can be calmer when discussing it.

4. Should I remind my partner to take a time-out when he is getting angry or abusive?

No. He is responsible for identifying his own feelings and taking the time-out. As long as you do it for him, he is *not* doing his job. If you are upset about his abuse, you take a time-out for yourself as long as you can do it safely. Remember, you cannot control another person's behavior, you can only protect yourself.

5. What should I do when he takes a time-out during a discussion?

Remind yourself that this is the first step—that it is better for him to take a time-out than to be abusive toward you. Waiting for him to return can lead to your feeling frustrated or abandoned. You can use the time in a time-out for yourself and then go about your regular business.

6. Would time-outs be useful for me?

Yes. If you find your own anger rising, a time-out is a tool you can use to calm down before trying to work out a conflict. However, your using time-outs for yourself will not necessarily change your partner's behaviors.

---

*Adapted with permission from the Family Violence Prevention Fund's publication entitled *Domestic Violence: A National Curriculum for Family Preservation Practitioners,* written by Susan Schecter, M.S.W., and Anne L. Ganley, Ph.D. May not be reproduced without permission.

Time-outs are good for you to use when you are in conflicts with your children or with other people. They are also good tools to teach children. Many schools and day care centers already use a form of time-outs as a way to help children to regulate their feelings and behaviors. The time-outs described here are somewhat different from those used with children.

I HAVE READ AND UNDERSTAND THE TIME-OUT PROCEDURES.

_____   _____   _____
Spouse or Partner's signature   Group Member's name (print)   Date

WHEN YOUR PARTNER BLOCKS YOUR PATH

 Handout

Sometimes, your partner will not cooperate with your attempts to take a time-out, no matter how respectfully you declare one. Here is a sequence that sometimes will occur:

1. You declare a time-out (following the steps correctly).

2. Your partner blocks your path so you cannot leave.

3. Now you should remind her of the time-out agreement that you have previously discussed.

4. But she continues to block your path.

5. Offer <u>her</u> the opportunity to leave instead of you, so she does not feel abandoned by you. For example, you might say, "OK, if you want to leave, that's cool too. I don't want you to feel like I'm leaving you. We just need a break right now until things calm down."

In this situation, you cannot afford to place any hands on your partner or to use any significant force to move her. Not only is this dangerous, but it is very likely that YOU will be arrested.

If none of these are successful in separating the two of you, you have three basic options:

I. Physical Escape
- Retreat through another exit (into a bathroom or a bedroom) and lock the door.
- Escape through a window if it is safe to do so.
- Agree to stay and discuss the situation until your partner relaxes and no longer blocks the door, then escape.

II. Calling for Help
- Dial 911. Explain that you have a history of domestic violence offenses and that your partner will not allow you to leave the premises. Make it clear that you are trying to avoid violence.
- Call someone who can talk to your partner and try to calm her down so that she cooperates with the time-out.
- Scream for help.

III. Staying Put
- Sit down and stay quiet. Repeat self-talk to yourself such as "It's not worth it to get into a fight" or "It's my job to stay calm now." Use relaxation techniques, like deep breathing, to help you stay calm.

None of these options are particularly great. They all contain significant risks, but they are designed to accomplish the most important goal in this situation: preventing both of you from getting hurt. We hope that you are never in this situation, but these are important strategies to keep in mind just in case.

RESPONSIBILITY PLAN

 **Handout**

TIME-OUT PLAN
What will tell you that you need to go?

-
-

Where will you go, what will you do?

-
-

GOOD FRIEND'S PHONE NUMBER

GROUP MEMBER'S PHONE NUMBER

```
EMERGENCY . . . . . . . . . . . . . . . . . . 911
CRISIS  LINE. . . . . . . . . .
CHILD  ABUSE . . . . . . . .
BATTERED  WOMEN. . . .
```

PREVIOUS PLANS
List three ways in the past that you have cooled down or controlled your anger:

-
-
-

PHYSICAL EXERCISE PLAN

STRESS MANAGEMENT PLAN
List three things that you enjoy doing, relax you, and help you think straight:

-
-
-

Session 3

ANGER, AGGRESSION, AND RED FLAGS

Materials:

> *Weekly Check-in*
> *"Understanding Anger"*
> *"Appropriate Alternatives to Violence"*
> *The Quieting Reflex* audiotape (or other similar relaxation tape)

Goals:

> To teach the men basic anger education and management skills; to encourage them not to use violence toward their partners; and to explore other options.

Tasks:

> 1. *Review Weekly Check-in.*
> 2. *Review homework.*
> 3. *Explain relaxation.*
> 4. *Play "The Quieting Reflex" tape.*
> 5. *Review "Understanding Anger."*
> 6. *Introduce concept of red flags.*
> 7. *Encourage discussion of anger and anger management, including modeling and role-play.*
> 8. *Assign homework.*

Program:

> 1. Letting Go to Gain Control: Relaxation Training (contributed by Daniel G. Saunders)
>
> Although aggression is not always preceded by anger, it often is. A necessary component of anger is physical arousal. Relaxation training is a way to reverse this arousal. It is also an important steppingstone to other skills in the program. Explain that learning to relax is a skill like any other.
>
> *Stress robs you of energy. The energy can be physical or emotional. If you let tension build in you, you are more likely to be irritable, to snap at your partner, or to feel down.*

Relaxation training can do a number of things for you. First, you can become more aware of body tension so you have a signal when anger or anxiety begins. Second, you can learn to keep some muscles very relaxed and other muscles tense, so you can save energy when you are physically active. This is why relaxation training is sometimes used by Olympic athletes. Third, you will probably find that having control over your muscle tension gives you more control over thoughts and feelings, like anger.

At first the training will take some practice. Later, relaxation becomes a habit for you. We do not intend for you to fall asleep. If you sleep, you will not develop true relaxation skills. Feel free, however, to let your mind go in whatever direction it wants during these experiences.

2. Play the 10-minute audiotape, *The Quieting Reflex* (or a similar relaxation tape). Discuss problems they might have had, for example, falling asleep or not wanting to keep their eyes closed. Discuss other forms of relaxation they might use, such as jogging or meditation.

3. Go over the handout "Understanding Anger." Ask the group members for their answers to each question. You might give some prompts, for example, asking how they know when their spouse is angry. Share examples from your own relationships or use your knowledge of other couples' experiences. Go into as much detail as necessary for explanation, clarification, or to meet specific men's needs. Model ways to deal effectively with anger. Have the men try role-playing an example. If time allows, go over the handout, "Appropriate Alternatives to Violence."

4. Introduce the concept of red flags. Explain how important it is to identify the warning signs of anger build-up. Refer to Commandment #5.

   - Physical red flags: muscle tension, heartbeat, disorientation, etc.
   - Red flag words: words that stir things up. What are the key phrases or words that can make someone "see red"? Where do they come from? School? Family? Friends?
   - Red flag situations: paying bills, hearing certain questions, dealing with kids. Which rooms set the stage for more conflict? Bedroom? Kitchen? Which rooms are most dangerous? (Probably the bathroom, because of the hard fixtures, and the kitchen because of the potential weapons.)
   - Red flag self-talk:

   "She's trying to make a fool of me."
   "She doesn't love me anymore."

5. Ask each group member to role-play a personal situation including all of the above types of red flags: physical, verbal, situations, self-talk. Make sure the other group members are genuinely convinced that they can "see" the red flags.

Homework

1. Read the handout on "Appropriate Alternatives to Violence." Choose two of the alternatives that you feel would be effective for you in dealing with anger. Record examples of how and when you used them.

UNDERSTANDING ANGER*

Handout

Anger is normal—but it tells us there is something wrong that needs changing. Too much anger can cause high blood pressure and other physical problems. The *behavior* that follows anger may not be normal; it may be very destructive, like physical violence, threats, verbally abusive comments, and sexual abuse.

Anger is always a secondary emotion. It follows something else, like frustration, extreme stress, feeling put down, or fearing rejection.

WHAT ARE THE SIGNS OF ANGER?

BODY:

- tense muscles
- sweating
- increased heart rate
- quickened breathing
- trembling
- face flushing

EMOTIONAL:

- tense
- agitated
- hurt
- outraged
- insulted

SELF-TALK:

- *"It's not fair."*
- *"I can't think straight!"*
- *"Nobody treats me like this!"*
- *"She deserves this!"*

WHAT DOES ANGER DO?

POSITIVE:

- Can be a "cue" to be assertive
- Motivates behavior
- Provides a creative, powerful source of energy

---

*Adapted with permission from Geffner & Mantooth, 1995. May not be reproduced without permission.

NEGATIVE:

- May lead to physical problems, illness
- Lowers self-esteem
- Creates work/relationship problems
- Results in behavioral problems, violence

WHAT ARE SOME WAYS TO DEAL WITH ANGER?

- Recognize the red flags: be aware of your body cues.
- Identify the source of the anger. Why are you angry?
- Deal with the situation or problem causing the anger.
- Talk to someone.
- Accept anger as normal—but remember that inappropriate behavior is not "normal."
- Sometimes it makes sense just to wait it out.

APPROPRIATE ALTERNATIVES TO VIOLENCE*

 Handout

1. **Jogging or Walking Briskly.** This is a benefit both for stress reduction and general health. When you feel good physically, you are able to confront stressful situations better. Also, the physical activity helps divert attention away from the stressful environment. A walk around the block is good for people who cannot jog.

2. **Physical Work.** Physical work can release energy in the same manner as jogging while at the same time getting something accomplished. The work can be at home or place of employment.

3. **Quiet Time.** This is getting off alone for a while. Listen to music, just sit quietly and daydream, or walk alone someplace that is restful, such as a park, lakeshore, woods, etc. You may also have a room at home where you can go to be away from everything for awhile.

4. **Deep Breaths.** Just stop for a minute when you feel tension and take some deep breaths. This adds oxygen to your body and helps you think more clearly, calm down, and shift your focus from the situation. Stretching or walking around while taking deep breaths helps.

5. **Talking.** Talking about the stress to another person is helpful. Talk about what is bothering you to someone whom you trust. If you are aware of the symptoms prior to anger and you talk about them instead of acting, it will help reduce your stress.

6. **Relaxation Procedures.** Tense and relax muscle groups, or use the "quieting reflex" from your relaxation tape.

---

*Adapted with permission from Geffner & Mantooth, 1995. May not be reproduced without permission.

Session 4

CYCLES OF ABUSE

Materials:

> *Weekly Check-in*
> *"The Cycle of Abuse"*
> *Brief Quieting Reflex* audiotape (or a similar relaxation tape)

Goal:

> To help the group members understand typical stages in family violence.

Tasks:

> 1. *Review Weekly Check-in.*
> 2. *Review homework.*
> 3. *Play Brief Quieting Reflex audiotape.*
> 4. *Explain "Cycle of Abuse" concept.*
> 5. *Assign homework.*

Program:

1. Practice relaxation training by playing the 5-minute *Brief Quieting Reflex* audiotape (or a similar relaxation tape).

2. Present the handout on the "Cycle of Abuse." The handout focuses on the three primary stages in the cycle of family violence: (1) tension-building (escalation); (2) violence (explosion); and (3) calm, loving (honeymoon). Explain to the men that this cycle is an accurate description of the pattern in *some* couples where abuse takes place. It is particularly helpful when working with women who have been abused, because it helps them see the patterns of behavior more clearly. However, not all couples follow this pattern. It is not inevitable that abusive behavior escalates. And not all men perceive this pattern as being the most accurate description of their own behavior. An alternative model, the Cycle of Feeling Avoidance, will be presented after this. It is better to address these issues up front to defuse resistance to this model.

3. First, present an overview of the three stages and ask the group members if they recognize some of the signs from each stage.

4. Next, discuss the tension-building stage. What are the cues and triggers that are likely to provoke the escalation? Review the red flags discussed in the previous group session.

5. Discuss the "withdrawal ritual" (Jacobson & Gottman, 1998a). Nonviolent couples employ this ritual so that at some point the escalation process stops or reverses itself. Some couples take breaks, other couples compromise, still others do both. In couples where severe battering takes place, women are often quite willing to stop at a point where they start to sense danger—but once the husbands are "activated," violence almost inevitably follows. Ask the men to think about any withdrawal rituals they and their wives already use. The goal here is to increase their awareness of successful strategies and of the red flags that typically signal disaster ahead.

6. Discuss the honeymoon phase. Here, the tables often turn, and the man who has been so domineering becomes very dependent. He recognizes how much he needs his partner and may often cling desperately. This stage can be extremely difficult for the partner to resist, because the vulnerable emotions are so appealing. In keeping with the basic principles of behavioral psychology, both partners may feel "reinforced" for the explosion. They may come to believe (unconsciously) that **this state can only be achieved in the aftermath of violence.**

Homework

1. Write down three red flag situations that have led you to be aggressive in the past.

2. Fill out "Alcohol & Other Substances Questionnaire." Prepare to discuss this in the group session next week.

The Cycle of Abuse

Handout

The Cycle of Abuse*

Tension Building		Acute Explosion		Remorse	
Abuser	**Victim's Response**	**Abuser**	**Victim's Response**	**Abuser**	**Victim's Response**
Moody	Attempts to calm partner	Hits	Protects him/herself	Apologizes/begs for forgiveness	Agrees to stay/return or take partner back
Nitpicking	Nurturing	Chokes	Calls Police	Sends flowers	Feels happy, hopeful
Violates partner	Silent/Talkative	Humiliates	Tries to calm abuser	Brings presents	Attempts to stop legal proceedings
Withdraws affection	Stays away from family/friends	Rapes	Tries to reason	Promises to get counseling/go to church/AA/etc.	Sets up counseling appointment for partner
Puts partner down	Keeps kids quiet	Uses weapons	Leaves	Wants to make love	
Yelling	Agrees	Beats	Fights back	Cries	
Drinking or drugs	Tries to reason	Restrains			
Threatens	General feeling of walking on eggshells	Pulls telephone out of wall			
Destroys property	Withdraws	Verbally abuses			
Criticizes					
Sullen					
Crazy-making					

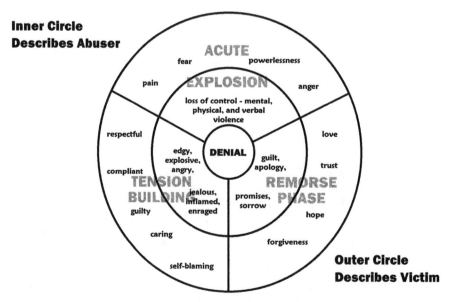

Inner Circle Describes Abuser

ACUTE EXPLOSION

fear   powerlessness

pain   anger

loss of control - mental, physical, and verbal violence

respectful   love

DENIAL

edgy, explosive, angry,   guilt, apology,   trust

compliant

TENSION BUILDING   jealous, inflamed, enraged   promises, sorrow   REMORSE PHASE

guilty   hope

caring   forgiveness

self-blaming

Outer Circle Describes Victim

Continued on following page...

* adapted with permission from Walker, L., 1984

The Cycle of Abuse... page 2

Denial

Denial works in each stage of the cycle to keep the cycle going. Only by breaking through this denial can the cycle be broken.

Tension Building

- **Victim** denies tension, or excuses it as resulting from outside stress, work, etc., or denies that the tension will worsen; victim blames self for own behavior.
- **Abuser** denies responsibility for actions by blaming the tension on partner, work, the traffic, drinking, etc.

Explosion

- **Victim** denies his/her injury, saying "it is only minor," "I bruise easily," "it didn't require police or medical help;" blames it on drinking; says "she/he didn't know what she/he was doing;" does not label it rape because it was her husband.
- **Abuser** blames it on partner, stress, etc.; says "she/he had it coming."

Remorse Phase

- **Victim** minimizes injuries by saying, "it could have been worse;" believes this is the way it will stay, believes partner's promises.
- **Abuser** also believes it won't happen again.

SELF-MANAGEMENT

Session 5

ALCOHOL AND OTHER SUBSTANCES: WHAT'S THE CONNECTION?

Materials:

> *Weekly Check-in*
> *"Alcohol & Other Substances and Abuse: What's the Connection?"*
> *"Alcohol & Other Substances Questionnaire"*
> *"Why Do I Use?"*
> *Brief Quieting Reflex* audiotape (or a similar relaxation tape)

Goal:

> To help each group member assess his own pattern of substance use and/or abuse and to identify the specific relationship between use of substances and relationship abuse.

Tasks:

> 1. *Review Weekly Check-in.*
> 2. *Review first part of homework.*
> 3. *Play Brief Quieting Reflex tape.*
> 4. *Discuss "Alcohol & Other Substances and Abuse: What's the Connection?"*
> 5. *Review "Alcohol & Other Substances Questionnaire."*
> 6. *Assign homework.*

Program:

1. Practice relaxation training by playing *Brief Quieting Reflex* audiotape (or a similar relaxation tape).

2. Most men who hurt the ones they love have problems with alcohol. Some also have problems with other drugs, like pot and cocaine. It is unlikely, however, that alcohol and other drugs *directly* cause aggression. Rather, the causal connection appears to be indirect, acting through the men's expectations, cultural norms, personality, mind set, and setting. And during withdrawal, the person may become irritable and liable to lash out. Long-term abuse may contribute to paranoia and subsequent proneness to aggression.

Some men who batter have a true addiction to alcohol or other drugs. Anyone who has relatives who are alcoholic should be told to be particularly cautious about drinking. It may be best to abstain from alcohol entirely. Blackouts are one sign of severe alcohol abuse. The men need to be made aware that, while drinking heavily, they may seriously hurt a loved one or a stranger and never remember the event. Society can still hold them responsible for their behavior while drunk, because they put themselves at risk by taking the first drink.

Explain that people use chemicals for many different reasons. Ask the men why they or others use chemicals and list their answers on the board.

Ask whether they think that alcohol physically causes aggression or whether alcohol and aggression are connected in other ways. List their responses on the board. Try to fit their responses into the following major theories:

a. **Physical Effects.** The physical properties of alcohol reduce the ability to control behavior, or it allows "stuffed" anger to come to the surface The chemicals have a "disinhibiting" effect.

b. **Social Learning.** Cultural attitudes teach that aggression and chemical abuse should go together: it is "macho" to drink alcohol and to be aggressive. Peer pressure can be especially strong on younger men.

c. **Excuse-making.** Before or after being aggressive, alcohol provides an excuse that others often accept. Rather than anger being "under the influence of alcohol," alcohol may be "under the influence of anger." A person may become angry and then decide to use alcohol to release his anger.

Explain that there is probably some truth to all of these theories. Stopping chemical abuse is likely to reduce the severity of aggression, but will not stop it altogether.

Discussion Questions:

1. Should people be held responsible for their actions while under the influence? If so, how?

2. Ask each group member whether he (and/or his partner) had consumed any alcohol (or other substances) during or prior to the incident that led to his coming to this treatment program. Ask group members to share a personal story of the destructive effects of alcohol or other substances in his life.

Homework

1. Fill out "Why Do I Use?"

ALCOHOL & OTHER SUBSTANCES AND ABUSE: WHAT'S THE CONNECTION?

H a n d o u t

Some people who hurt the ones they love have problems with alcohol. Some also have problems with other drugs, like pot, crack, and cocaine. Ours is a culture that often encourages the abuse of alcohol and the display of aggression under this influence. Consequently, people under the influence sometimes do things impulsively they may not ordinarily do, and their judgment and control are impaired.

People use chemicals for many different reasons. On the questionnaires that follow, think about the reasons that you use alcohol or drugs. Then, identify whether alcohol or other drugs impair your judgment or cause you to become aggressive. Many people identify these themes as they think about these questions:

1. **Social Drinking.** There may be peer pressure and/or cultural pressure to abuse alcohol. Commercials even emphasize "Why ask 'Why?' Have another beer."

2. **Habit.** Many people equate socializing with alcohol use. Others believe the only way to unwind is through drinking. Drinking becomes routine.

3. **Psychological Dependency.** When alcohol use is well established, it's hard to imagine doing without it. Perhaps by this stage, temporary attempts have been made to abstain.

4. **Physical Dependency.** Once the person is physically addicted, withdrawal can have severe effects. By that time, medical, legal, vocational, and family problems attributed to alcohol abuse likely have probably signaled a problem.

Have you ever conducted yourself under the influence in ways you have later regretted?

Have you ever experienced memory lapses or "blackouts"?

Have you ever been told that you have an alcohol problem?

Any "yes" answers indicate that alcohol use has probably impaired your ability to be fully in control of your life. Remember the 100% rule regarding responsibility. Alcohol problems are progressive—without help, they get worse. Can you really be 100% committed to being in control of your life and still continue to use alcohol or drugs?

ALCOHOL & OTHER SUBSTANCES QUESTIONNAIRE

 **Handout**

1. How often do you use alcohol or other drugs?
   a. Never
   b. Once every few months
   c. At least once a month
   d. At least once a week
   e. A few times a week
   f. Every day

2. What are the main reasons that you use alcohol or drugs?
   a.

   b.

   c.

3. What are the main "cues" for drinking or using drugs?
   a. Which people?

   b. Which places?

   c. What life events or situations (parties, work stress, sports games, etc.)?

   d. What emotions (sadness, anger, celebration, etc.)?

   e. What self-talk ("This isn't fair," "I deserve this," "It's time to have fun," "Nobody can control me," etc.)

4. Name one time when you became more abusive or aggressive when using alcohol or drugs.

5. Has anyone ever told you that your alcohol or drug use is a problem?

WHY DO I USE?

 **Handout**

Think about the reasons that you use (or abuse) alcohol or other substances. Even if your use does not cause many problems in your life, it still serves some purpose. Check off on the list below the different reasons for your use of alcohol or other substances. We will discuss these in the next group session.

____ To relax
____ To feel more at ease in social situations
____ Just because it tastes good
____ Because my friends expect me to
____ To have fun
____ To avoid other people
____ To feel more relaxed about having sex
____ To avoid bad feelings (depression, anxiety, loneliness, etc.)
____ To avoid feeling angry
____ To have an excuse for getting rowdy
____ To have an excuse for getting my anger out
____ To feel better about myself
____ To stop worrying about problems
____ To get a little buzzed
____ To get drunk
____ To go to sleep

Session 6

SELF-TALK AND BAD RAP

Materials:

> *Weekly Check-in*
> *"Bad Rap"*
> *"Bad Rap Quiz"*
> *"Examples of Anger-Producing Self-Talk"*

Goals:

> To introduce group members to the basic concept of self-talk and to increase aware-ness of how interpretations of events can determine feelings and reactions.

Tasks:

> 1. *Review Weekly Check-in.*
> 2. *Review homework.*
> 3. *Explain concept of self-talk through ABCDE model.*
> 4. *Explain and discuss categories of "Bad Rap."*
> 5. *Conduct "Bad Rap Quiz."*
> 6. *Review "Examples of Anger-Producing Self-talk."*
> 7. *Assign homework.*

Program:

1. Introduce a basic working model of "self-talk." Use the ABCDE model (explained below), emphasizing how the way we interpret events can determine the way we feel and act (from Wexler, 1991a).

   a. **Objective Event**: This is the initial event. Your wife or partner comes home and says, *"I hate my job!"*

   b. **Self-Talk**: You might say to yourself: *"She's trying to tell me that she doesn't want to work and that I should be making more money so she shouldn't have to!"*

   c. **Feelings and Behavior**: If you interpreted it this way, you would probably be critical of her, or act defensive, or sulk, or worry. Maybe you would say to her: *"Quit complaining! You think you're the only one who has it tough?"*

    d. **New Self-Talk:** Maybe there was another way to interpret what she said. Maybe she was just tired and needed some support, like we all do. Maybe it was not intended as a message or critical comment. You might be saying to yourself, *"She sounds like she's had a rotten day. What can I do to help?"*

    e. **New Feelings and Behavior:** If you interpreted it this way, you might say: *"Let's talk about it."* Or you might try to cheer her up. Or you might just whisk the kids off into another room and let her be alone for a while. Your response would be based on what you thought she might need, rather than defending yourself against a perceived attack.

2. Now explain the seven categories of "Bad Rap." Teach the names of the categories and go through the different examples. Ask the group members to come up with examples of their own.

3. Quiz group members with the "Bad Rap Quiz," to make sure that they get the idea. Try turning this into a Family Feud contest, with different teams competing for the right answer. If one team identifies the correct category for the statement, award a point. This team then has the opportunity to rephrase the statement so that it reflects "productive" or "realistic" self-talk, worth an additional point. If a team answers incorrectly, the other team can try, until one of the teams gets it right. Make sure that they learn how to revise the "faulty" self-talk into sentences that would be more "realistic" self-talk.

4. Explain the following example:

> *There is one person whom we talk with more than any other person and who has more influence over us than anyone else. Sometimes we argue with that person and sometimes we simply follow the demands made on us. That person is our self. Conversations with ourselves are often hidden and can happen very quickly. Even though they are hidden, they can make the difference between a happy and miserable life.*
>
> *Imagine the following situation: A coworker greets you with a happy "hello" every morning. This morning, though, he frowns and grumbles "hello." If you tend to take things personally, you might immediately think that he is upset with you and become hurt, angry, or both. However, if you learned that he was recovering from an illness and was still not feeling well, you might reach a very different conclusion. Jumping to conclusions is one of the common ways we create our own anger. To give another example, without any concrete evidence, Ed started worrying that his wife Carolyn would leave him. When he thought about it, his mind would race:*
>
> *"Can I live without her? I don't know. I'd better be strong. She won't respect me if I'm not strong. She probably never loved me to begin with—she only wanted me to give her children." As you can imagine, Ed ended up feeling sad and bitter and he was unable to tell anyone about it. He kept asking her for signs of her love, but his constant asking began to drive her away.*

5. Explain "Examples of Anger-Producing Self-Talk" and discuss.

Homework

1. Record three examples of "bad rap" over the next week. Write down the self-talk, the category of "bad rap," and new self-talk that would have been more realistic or productive.

BAD RAP*

Handout

1. **BLACK & WHITE:** Seeing things as all or nothing. Beware of words like "never," "always," "nothing," and "everyone."

   "Real men don't admit their mistakes."
   "You're either on my side or you're not."
   "You can't trust anyone over 30."

2. **MINIMIZING:** Downplaying your achievements.

   "Even though I finally made supervisor, it's no big deal."
   "I did well, but so did a lot of other people."
   "My counselor just gives me good feedback because she's paid to say it."

3. **MINDREADING:** Assuming that others think something without checking it out.

   "I know my boss hates me—he gave me a dirty look."
   "She's avoiding me—she must be pretty mad."
   "My girlfriend didn't call me today–she must not care about me."

4. **AWFULIZING:** Predicting that things will turn out "awful" for you.

   "My boss will never trust me again."
   "I know I'm not going to make it through this place."
   "Wow, he is so good at that—I'll never be able to do it that well!"

5. **ERROR IN BLAMING:** Unfairly blaming yourself—or others.

   "It's all my fault," or "It's all their fault."
   "It's my fault my son is shy."
   "You always mess everything up for me."

6. **DOWN-PUTTING:** Making too much of your shortcomings or mistakes (the opposite of **MINIMIZING**).

   "I'm overweight, so I must be lazy and stupid."
   "I failed this test; I must be dumb."
   "I'm in counseling; I must be a bad person."
   "She doesn't like me; I must be ugly."

7. **EMOTIONAL REASONING:** Concluding that if you feel a certain way about yourself, then it must be true.

   "Since I feel bad about myself, I must be a bad person."
   "I feel rejected, so everybody must be rejecting me."
   "Since I feel guilty, I must have done something wrong."

---

*Adapted with permission from Wexler, 1991b. May not be reproduced without permission.

BAD RAP QUIZ*

 **Handout**

1. The counselor told me I'm doing better, but I know he tells that to everybody.

2. Ever since Linda hurt me, I know redheads can't be trusted.

3. Nothing's ever going to work out for me.

4. It's your fault we never do anything fun.

5. My parents got divorced—it must have been something about me.

6. I sometimes don't get things right so I must be lazy or stupid.

7. I feel lonely, so I guess nobody likes me.

8. That supervisor shows me no respect—nobody in this organization cares a damn about me.

---

*Adapted with permission from Wexler, 1991b. May not be reproduced without permission.

EXAMPLES OF ANGER-PRODUCING SELF-TALK*

 **Handout**

She called me a name.
She doesn't show me respect.
I have to protect my honor.
I will show her what it feels like by calling her a name.
I have a right to pay her back for what she has done to me.

****

I see her talking with another man.
They are probably attracted toward each other.
I have to watch my wife; I can't let her be tempted.
She wants him and she doesn't want me.
She is my wife and this is humiliating to me.
She is a bad person.
She has hurt me and I have to pay her back.
I will make sure she knows what she has done, and I'll hurt her as much as she has hurt me—*whatever it takes.*

*Thanks to Daniel G. Saunders, Ph.D. for this technique. May not be reproduced without permission.

Session 7

USING SELF-TALK FOR ANGER

Materials:

> *Weekly Check-in*
> *Compassion videotape*
> *"HEALS"*
> *"Self-talk for Anger Management"*
> *"Anger Ladder"*

Goal:

> To use the self-talk skills to prepare for anger-producing situations and to cope more effectively.

Tasks:

> 1. **Review Weekly Check-in.**
> 2. **Review homework.**
> 3. **Review basic principles of self-talk.**
> 4. **Play the Compassion videotape. Review "HEALS" and discuss.**
> 5. **Introduce "Self-talk for Anger Management."**
> 6. **Review specific "Self-talk for Anger Management" plan for one group member.**
> 7. **Role-play this plan.**
> 8. **Explain "Anger Ladder" and assign homework.**

Program:

1. Review the basic principles of self-talk. Reemphasize how interpretations of events play a powerful role in determining our emotions and reactions.

2. Play the *Compassion* tape. Explain the "HEALS" technique by reviewing the handout. Role-play situations in which the men could have used this technique. Remind the men that they are free to choose their own words or phrases as long as they follow the basic principles of the "HEALS" technique. Be prepared for resistance to the idea of showing so much compassion to the person who *appears* to be the source of one's hurt and anger.

3. Introduce the four-step model of "Self-talk for Anger Management." Use the handout to provide examples of self-statements that can be used to lower stress levels at each of these stages. The fourth step can be just as important as the others, even though it takes place after the incident. Be sure that they understand the importance of using realistic and supportive self-talk during this final stage also.

4. Ask one group member to identify a potential anger situation and to generate self-statements for each of the four stages. The more unique and personalized the statements the better.

5. Role-play this situation with this group member, practicing both the old and the new self-talk. Focus on the different feelings that result from the new self-talk.

6. In preparation for the "Anger Ladder" homework, construct some Anger Ladders on the board with examples from one of the men. Anger Ladders are made up of scenes associated with anxiety or anger. Introduce this concept by telling the group members that it is very important to understand the different shades and levels of anger.

The following is an example of an Anger Ladder:

5. You learn that your wife or partner is having an affair (*highest rung on Anger Ladder*).
4. You are laid off work.
3. Your partner calls you a "lazy jerk."
2. One of your co-workers criticizes you.
1. You have trouble finding one of your shoes and you get to work two minutes late (*lowest rung on the Anger Ladder*).

Homework

1. The Anger Ladder will be used to help you overcome the stress associated with anger. Please list below next to the number 5 the situation that has or would make you the most angry. Next, list the situation after the number 1 that has or would make you the least angry. Then fill in the situations from 2 through 4 showing increasing levels of anger.

   5.
   4.
   3.
   2.
   1.

2. Work on a specific Self-talk for Anger Management plan and bring it in next week. Pick a situation that you know puts you at risk for becoming angry. The plan should include one example of self-talk for each of the four different stages.

3. Record three examples of using the HEALS technique. Record the situation, the core uncomfortable feeling you identified, and the compassionate statements toward yourself and toward your wife or partner. MAKE SURE TO SPEND THE FULL 20 SECONDS FEELING THE CORE UNCOMFORTABLE FEELING.

   - Situation:
   - Core Uncomfortable Feeling:
   - Compassionate Statements:
     - Toward Myself:
     - Toward Her:

HEALS*

Handout

1. **HEALING.** When you feel your anger rising toward your wife or partner, turn away from her and turn to yourself. See the letters flash in bright lights: HEALING. Say to yourself: "I need to heal, not hurt." Or feel free to choose your own word or phrase. Blame is powerless, but compassion is true power, and has the ability to heal. Anger numbs the pain of the core hurts, but it prevents them from healing.

2. **EXPLAIN** to yourself the core hurt that anger is masking: feeling unimportant, disregarded, guilty, devalued, rejected, powerless, and unlovable.

   - *I saw her talking to him and I felt like I didn't count. It didn't matter to her what I felt!*
   - *I felt disregarded. I felt unimportant.*
   - *I felt accused, and I suddenly saw myself as being a jealous asshole.*
   - *I felt rejected.*
   - *I couldn't stop her from talking to him and I felt unlovable.*
   - *I felt powerless.*
   - *No one can love me with these kinds of feelings.*

   Much abusive behavior is motivated by these core hurts. Say slowly: *"I feel unlovable."* Feel it for 20 seconds.

3. **APPLY COMPASSION:**

   a. Offer compassion to yourself.
      - *I know I am lovable.*
      - *I can learn from this.*
      - *I know I have something to offer.*
      - *I know I'm an important person.*

   b. Offer compassion to your partner.
      - *It's not rejection of how I was just now, it's rejection of how I was in the past.*
      - *I need to understand her.*
      - *I need to give her time.*

4. **LOVE YOURSELF** by feeling compassion. See yourself as important, valuable, internally powerful, worthy of respect, lovable: "I *know* I am lovable."

5. **SOLVE THE PROBLEM.** Present your true position without blaming or attacking her: *"I care about you, but I have a problem with what you said to me."* Or, in some cases, say nothing at all, and take care of these feelings internally or by talking to another person. You are healing your core hurt through love rather than anger.

---

*Adapted with permission from Stosny, 1995. May not be reproduced without permission.

SELF-TALK FOR ANGER MANAGEMENT*

 **Handout**

READY

This could be a rough situation, but I know how to deal with it. I can work out a plan to handle this. Easy does it. Remember, stick to the issues and don't take it personally. There won't be any need for an argument. I know what to do.

SET

As long as I keep my cool, I'm in control of the situation. I don't need to prove myself. I don't want to make more of this than I have to. There is no point in getting mad. I've got to think of what I have to do. Look for positives and don't jump to conclusions.

GO

Muscles are getting tight. Relax and slow things down. Time to take a deep breath. Let's take the issue point by point. My anger is a signal of what I need to do. Time for problem-solving. She might want me to get angry, but I'm going to deal with it constructively.

EVALUATION

1. *Rocky Waters*
Forget about the aggravation. Thinking about it only makes me upset. Try to shake it off. Don't let it interfere with the job. Remember relaxation. It's a lot better than anger. Don't take it personally. It's probably not so serious.

2. *Smooth Sailing*
I handled that one pretty well. That's doing a good job. I could have gotten more upset than it was worth. My pride can get me into trouble, but I'm doing better at this all the time. I actually got through this without getting angry.

---

*Adapted with permission from Novaco, 1979. May not be reproduced without permission.

ANGER LADDER*

Handout

The Anger Ladder will help you overcome the stress associated with anger.

Please list below next to the number 5 the situation that has or would make you the most angry. Next, list the situation after the number 1 that has or would make you the least angry. Then fill in the situations from 2 through 4, showing increasing levels of anger.

Your counselor or group leader will use these anger-producing scenes in combination with relaxation to help you overcome stress and anger.

5. Extremely angry, about to explode: _____

_____

_____

_____

4. _____

_____

_____

_____

3. Moderate anger, can notice tension: _____

_____

_____

_____

2. _____

_____

_____

_____

1. Low anger, mild irritation: _____

_____

_____

_____

Session 8
SELF-ESTEEM

Materials:

> *Weekly Check-in*
> *Anger Ladder* audiotape
> *"House of Self-worth & Empowerment"*

Goal:

> To offer the men ways of changing self-esteem through self-awareness, cognitive restructuring, or lifestyle modification.

Tasks:

> 1. *Review Weekly Check-in.*
> 2. *Play Anger Ladder audiotape and review.*
> 3. *Review homework.*
> 4. *Review criteria for progress from Evaluation Form; discuss self-assessment.*
> 5. *Conduct exercise on "What's The Worst You Call Yourself?"*
> 6. *Discuss "House of Self-Worth & Empowerment."*
> 7. *Ask group members to say something positive about themselves.*
> 8. *Assign homework.*

Program:

> 1. Write the Anger Ladders constructed in the last session on the board. Tell the group members that, after the relaxation exercise on the tape, they will be asked to imagine a tense scene. Tell them to use the lowest scene on their ladder. Review the low scenes to make sure they are appropriately low. Now play the *Anger Ladder* audiotape.
>
>   Instruct the men to go up one rung of the Anger Ladder in the next session (to a more tense scene), only if the tense scene became less tense over the three times it was presented here. Only the three lowest scenes will be used over the course of three sessions.

2. Review the Evaluation Form that you will be using to evaluate group members' performance. Explain each of the criteria. Although this has already been reviewed during their initial orientation, make it clear that you repeat this so they will be fully informed about what you value and look for in this program. As you review each item, ask at least one group member to assess his own performance in this area. This is an excellent opportunity to offer genuine feedback, bolster self-esteem, and stimulate increased mutual support from group members.

3. What's the Worst You Call Yourself?: People often react strongly to criticism because they are already strongly criticizing themselves. By being more aware of the worst things we call ourselves or fear that someone else might call us, we can defuse the impact of the criticism.

Explain that by talking about "weak spots" in ourselves or ways we put ourselves down, we can start to feel better. Sometimes we take in what was said about us as kids and totally believe it. Talking about it gives us some distance from it. We are not so likely to be hurt as when we were kids.

Ask the men to share some of the ways they put themselves down with labels, for example: *"I'm stupid," "I'm a fuck up," "I'm just lazy,"* etc. Caution them not to reveal more than they feel comfortable revealing. Ask if they know when someone else might have called them that name. Ask if they are willing to tell what they would fear being called by someone else.

4. Reinforce the importance of positive self-esteem and talk about how self-esteem can be changed. Discuss the "House of Self-Worth & Empowerment" by drawing the house on the board, much like the "House of Abuse" from Session 1. Ask the group members to generate information about areas of their lives that are important to them and that provide them with experiences of self-worth. As with the "House of Abuse" the specific ideas should be clustered into different rooms of the house. Although these room names can be altered according to the particular group, suggested room names are the following:

- Job
- Social Life
- Relaxation
- Parenting
- Spirituality
- Wife/Partner Relationship
- Personal Skills (Athletics, Manual Skills, Intellectual Abilities, etc.)
- Personal Integrity (examples of "doing the right thing")

Then start asking the questions:

- How does it feel to live in this House?
- How do the rooms strengthen each other?
- What do you need to do to make sure that these rooms are filled?

And, the final question:

- What do these rooms support? What is on the roof?

The answer is "self-worth" and "empowerment."

4. A good group activity at this time is to have each group member say something positive about himself. This can aid the bonding process as well as build self-esteem. Discuss any unusual reactions, and be sure to check out the person's feelings about what was said about him.

Homework

1. Make a list of (a) five positive traits in yourself and (b) five personal accomplishments.

THE HOUSE OF SELF-WORTH & EMPOWERMENT*

 Handout

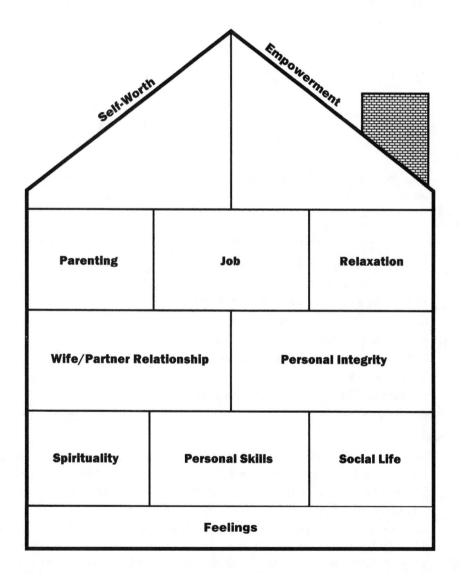

The House of Self-Worth & Empowerment

*The House of Self-Worth & Empowerment chart was developed by the staff of the Community Assistance Program (CAP) of the Amherst H. Wilder Foundation and is used here by permission. The chart is part of a complete domestic abuse curriculum entitled Foundations for Violence-Free Living: A Step-by-Step Guide to Facilitating Men's Domestic Abuse Groups, available from the Wilder Publishing Center at 1-800-274-6024.

Session 9

FEELINGS: PROPER CARE AND FEEDING

Materials:

> *Weekly Check-in*
> *Anger Ladder* audiotape
> *"The Feelings List"*

Goal:

> To help the group members identify a wide range of feelings and develop new ways of handling difficult ones.

Tasks:

> 1. *Review Weekly Check-in.*
> 2. *Review homework.*
> 3. *Play Anger Ladder audiotape and review.*
> 4. *Discuss the "macho" role for men.*
> 5. *Introduce concept of feelings.*
> 6. *List the primary feelings on the board.*
> 7. *Review "The Feelings List."*
> 8. *Explain "Cycle of Intolerable Feelings" concept.*

Program:

1. Write individual examples of Anger Ladder items from the *second* lowest scene on their ladder. Tell the group members that, after the relaxation exercise on the tape, they will be asked to imagine a tense scene. Review the scenes to make sure they are appropriate. Now play the *Anger Ladder* audiotape.

2. Men cut themselves off from a full range of feelings because of their socialization into a "macho" role. In general, it is difficult for men to know themselves, much less to express themselves to others. It is not the case, as many women assume, that men do not have feelings. What happens is that the softer feelings of hurt and fear become quickly converted into anger and then into aggression. Men feel, but often it isn't obvious to themselves or to others.

Explain that men often cheat themselves by not knowing themselves fully. Our tendency to hold in the "soft" emotions or to act out our "tough" ones helps to explain why men on average die seven years earlier than women. A common fear is that if men express their hurt or fear the other person will "use it against us." In a close relationship, just the opposite usually happens.

Explain the following: *Feelings are emotional states. There are four primary feelings: sadness, joy, fear, and anger. Many people include a fifth category, known as shame or humiliation. Just as the primary colors have many shades and mixtures, so there are many shades and mixtures of feelings. Feelings are different from thoughts, opinions, and beliefs. "I feel you put me down" is an opinion or observation. "I felt hurt when you said that" combines a feeling statement with an observation.*

3. List the five primary feelings across the top of the board. Ask the men to name similar feelings under the primary ones. Point out the range of intensity in the examples given. Emphasize the importance of expressing feelings when they first arise—at low intensity.

4. Review "The Feelings List." Ask a group member to pick out one of the emotions from the list—and then act it out. The rest of the group should guess the emotion. Continue on with each group member choosing a different item on the list. This should be fun—and should help the group members clarify labels for different emotions.

5. Ask the following: *What feelings were you punished for having as a child? What positive things can you tell yourself when you show hurt or fear?*

6. Now present the "Cycle of Intolerable Feelings" (Harway & Evans, 1996) handout. Explain that this is the way men often experience the build-up of anger and explosiveness. According to this model, when a man experiences unbearable feelings—like hurt, shame, helplessness, fear, guilt, inadequacy, and loneliness—he frequently feels overwhelmed. He has been taught that these are bad feelings and signs of weakness. So he needs to defend against these feelings, although these defenses do not provide much of a solution:

   - denying responsibility and placing blame on her: *"Why do you make me feel so bad about myself?"*
   - controlling everything and everyone in the vicinity: *"I want you all to get out of your rooms and clean up this house now—or else!"*
   - using alcohol or drugs to temporarily take away the pain
   - seeking excitement to distract from the bad feelings: *"I'm going to go get laid by someone who really knows how to make a man feel good!"*

When these defenses provide relief, they are reinforced as behavioral options. This cycle lives within the batterer. Although, of course, some event typically triggers a reaction, he (or she) is the one who must learn to tolerate a wider range of negative affect without acting out.

THE FEELINGS LIST

Handout

Below is a list of some of the more common feelings. The list could go on for pages. The only way most of us (particularly men) learn about how to label our different feelings is by being around other people who give us some feedback.

For example, when you were a baby, you didn't know the names of the different colors. Someone kept telling you that the sky was blue and that the fire engine was red. You learned, after more practice, that red had many different shades: scarlet is different from pink, and maroon is not quite the same as burgundy.

The same is true for feelings. Many men feel upset inside and label it "pissed." But different levels and shades of anger may range from irritated and frustrated to furious and enraged. Furthermore, feelings "pissed" is often a man's way of saying that he is really feeling hurt, threatened, or ashamed.

- excited
- tender
- sad
- lonely
- edgy
- frustrated
- frightened
- contented
- depressed
- timid
- hurt
- jealous
- loving
- elated
- happy

See if you can classify these in one of the five major categories. Some may not fit neatly into only one category.

The more familiar you are with these different feelings, the more power you have over your own experience and reactions.

Self-knowledge is power.

THE CYCLE OF INTOLERABLE FEELINGS*

 Handout

The Cycle of Intolerable Feelings*

Tension
(from unacceptable feelings)

- helpless
- hurt
- ashamed
- incompetent
- insignificant

Problems

Defense Against Feeling

(Passive)   **(Active)**

- placating
- apologizing
- seducing

- blaming others
- violence/abuse
- controlling others
- alcohol & drugs
- seeking excitement
- withdrawing emotionally

Relief

*Adapted from Harway & Evans, 1996

Session 10
MASCULINITY TRAPS I

Materials:

> *Weekly Check-in*
> *Anger Ladder* audiotape
> *The Great Santini* videotape: *Scene I*
> *"Masculinity Traps"*

Goal:

To increase awareness of how self-talk about "being a man" can be destructive and lead to violent behavior.

Tasks:

1. *Review Weekly Check-in.*
2. *Play Anger Ladder audiotape and review.*
3. *Discuss concept of self-talk and masculinity traps.*
4. *Give examples of masculinity traps.*
5. *Play The Great Santini videotape: Scene I. Discuss.*
6. *Review "Masculinity Traps" and discuss.*
7. *Discuss ways in which men have been encouraged or trained to be violent.*
8. *Assign homework.*

Program:

1. Write individual examples of Anger Ladder items from the *third* lowest scene on their ladder. Tell the group members that, after the relaxation exercise on the tape, they will be asked to imagine a tense scene. Review the scenes to make sure they are appropriate. Now play the *Anger Ladder* audiotape.

2. Explain that men engage in certain types of self-talk because of the roles in which they are placed. The primary roles, called "masculinity traps," are beliefs (a) that we have to be in charge, (b) that we must always win, and (c) that we must always be "cool" and not express our feelings.

3. Play *The Great Santini* videotape: Scene I (begin at 1:03:22 and end at 1:12:18). Discuss the ways in which the son has become oppressed by his father's warped attitudes about masculinity.

4. Review the "Masculinity Traps" handout. Encourage discussion using the following questions:

   - How were you encouraged to be competitive, tough, and aggressive?
   - Have you thought about or actually acted out violent pornography?
   - How were you encouraged to be tough?
   - How do you know when you are a man?
   - What messages were different for boys and girls in your family?

Homework

As you review the self-talk that represents masculinity traps, write your answers to the following questions:

1. Which of these beliefs do your recognize in yourself?

2. Would you like your son to grow up with these beliefs? Why not?

3. How do men suffer when they are stuck with these beliefs?

4. Would you like to be friends with men who think like this?

MASCULINITY TRAPS*

 **Handout**

As you review the self-talk that represents masculinity traps, ask yourself the following questions:

1. Which of these beliefs do you recognize in yourself?

2. Would you like your son to grow up with these beliefs? Why not?

3. How do men suffer when they are stuck with these beliefs?

4. Would you like to be friends with men who think like this?

"I can never show my feelings. Always be tough."
"Never show any weakness."
"Never do anything 'feminine.'"
"I have to be in control at all times."

"I must win."
"Winning is all."
"I must be successful at everything!"
"Don't back down from a fight."
"Always try to win arguments."
"Be on top by finding fault in others."
"Real men solve problems by force."

"My possessions and success are the measure of who I am."
"My value equals my paycheck."
"My car and my clothes and my house prove what kind of man I am."

*Adapted with permission from Daniel G. Saunders. May not be reproduced without permission.

Session 11
MASCULINITY TRAPS II

Materials:

Weekly Check-in
Men's Work videotape: Scene I
"Men Are Supposed to . . ."
Men's Work videotape: Scene II
"Rights as a Man"

Goals:

To increase awareness of how self-talk about "being a man" can be destructive and to help develop awareness of new bystander options.

Tasks:

1. *Review Weekly Check-in.*
2. *Review homework.*
3. *Play Anger Ladder tape and discuss.*
4. *Play Men's Work videotape: Scene I.*
5. *Lead group members through written "Men Are Supposed to . . ." exercise.*
6. *Continue Men's Work videotape: Scene I.*
7. *Discuss responses.*
8. *Play Men's Work videotape: Scene II.*
9. *Discuss self-talk and bystander issues.*
10. *Review "Rights as a Man."*

Program:

1. Play the *Men's Work* videotape: Scene I (begin at 2:07 and end at 11:57). Take a break at the point at which the exercise about "Men Are Supposed to . . ." appears on the screen. The screen will say STOP TAPE. Ask each of the group members to fill out the "Men Are Supposed to . . ." information. Return to the *Men's Work* videotape and listen to the examples that the actors recite. Generate a group discussion about these issues.

2. Play the *Men's Work* videotape: Scene II (begin at **19:16** and end at **23:42**), the vignette in which the man abuses his wife after a frustrating day at work. Continue through to his discussion with male neighbor. Review with group members the ways in which this scene may be familiar. Review the self-talk of the male. Consider alternatives for how else he may have been able to handle this.

3. Review reactions to the intervention from the other man. Discuss bystander issues.

    - How does a "real man" act in situations when he observes another male behaving badly?
    - What options does the bystander man have in these situations?
    - How would this change if you knew the woman personally?
    - What if this were your sister?
    - Is it an example of loyalty to ignore it?
    - Would it be different if you didn't like her?

4. Review "Rights as a Man." Discuss ways in which it might be threatening to give up the "masculinity trap" self-talk.

MEN ARE SUPPOSED TO . . .

 **Handout**

Men are supposed to be . . .

-
-
-
-

Men are supposed to do . . .

-
-
-
-

Men are supposed to have . . .

-
-
-
-

Men are *not* supposed to . . .

-
-
-
-

RIGHTS AS A MAN*

 **Handout**

1. *As a man*, I have the right to show my feelings and express my fears.

2. *As a man*, I have the right to change and the right to choose the direction of my change.

3. *As a man*, I can ask for help when I need it and offer help when I think it is needed.

4. *As a man*, I have the right to ask for what I want and the wisdom to know that I cannot always get it.

5. *As a man*, I have the right to tell people when I cannot fulfill their expectations of me.

6. *As a man*, I have the right to consider new ways of thinking, acting, and relating to people.

7. *As a man*, I am not obliged to live up to the stereotypes of how I am "supposed" to be.

8. *As a man*, I have the right to acknowledge my frustrations, disappointments, and anxieties.

9. *As a man*, I can choose to take responsibility for my actions and not allow other people's behavior to push me into choices I do not want to make.

10. *As a man*, I have the right to show my strength by choosing not to hit someone who angers me.

---

*Adapted with permission from Wachter & Boyd, 1982. May not be reproduced without permission.

Session 12
JEALOUSY AND MISINTERPRETATIONS

Materials:

> *Weekly Check-in*
> *"Jealousy: Taming the Green-Eyed Monster"*
> *"Misinterpretations"*

Goal:

> To help men understand the ways their jealous reactions can trigger violent behavior.

Tasks:

> 1. *Review Weekly Check-in.*
> 2. *Introduce concept of self-talk and jealousy.*
> 3. *Review the handout on "Jealousy."*
> 4. *Write summary of the four lessons at the end of the handout.*
> 5. *Discuss jealousy experiences.*
> 6. *Review "Misinterpretations."*
> 7. *Assign homework and introduce ideas about "put-downs."*

Program:

1. One of the strongest, most consistent traits of men who batter is jealousy. Sometimes the jealousy is based on reality and sometimes it is entirely fantasy—stemming from the insecurity of the man or his use of alcohol or other drugs. The skills learned thus far can be applied to keeping jealous feelings at a manageable level. An important perspective to convey is that jealousy arises from cultural norms.

2. Explain the points made in the first part of the handout "Jealousy: Taming the Green-Eyed Monster."

   Jealousy is one of those emotions that can tie our stomachs in knots in a hurry. A little bit of jealousy is natural, especially when we fear losing someone close to us. Jealousy becomes a problem when we spend too much energy worrying about losing a loved one, when we let jealousy build and we try to control another through aggression, or when we stifle a relationship by placing restrictions on our partners.

101

Read the stories from the handout. Write a summary of the four lessons at the end of the handout on the board.

Discussion questions:

- Have you had thoughts or feelings similar to any of the people in the stories?
- What have you found that works to reduce jealousy?
- What constructive self-talk can you use to combat jealousy?
- How would you respectfully ask your partner to contract for behavior change to reduce jealousy?

3. Review "Misinterpretations." Discuss the wide range of possible self-talk in response to the vignettes and how different outcomes and behaviors inevitably follow.

4. When presenting "Put-downs from Parents" as homework for the next session, spend 5–10 minutes discussing specific *personal* examples of put-downs you experienced or that others in your family experienced. Also, suggest that the men add other examples that are not on the scale, such as the put-down a man experiences when his father abandons him. Normalize this experience as much as possible.

Homework

1. Record three experiences of jealousy over the next week. These can include anything from high levels (like seeing your wife or partner flirting with another man) to low (like observing your supervisor give approval to someone else). If you do not notice any this week, recall experiences from previous weeks.

2. Complete "Put-downs from Parents." This handout will not be scored. Rather, it will be used in the next group session to help group members discuss how put-downs from the past affect self-talk in the present.

JEALOUSY: TAMING THE GREEN-EYED MONSTER*

 **Handout**

Jealousy is one of those emotions that can tie our stomach in knots in a hurry. A little bit of jealousy is natural, especially when we fear losing someone close to us. Jealousy becomes a problem

- when we spend too much energy worrying about losing a loved one
- when we let jealousy build and we try to control someone else through aggression
- when we stifle a relationship by placing extreme restrictions on our partner

  ✳ Pete got himself really worked up whenever he went to a party with his wife, Sue. It seemed that she was attracted to some of the other men and they were apparently attracted to her. Deep inside he was afraid that she would find another man more attractive and exciting than he was. He feared losing her love. But what usually happened was a fight after the party, a fight not about jealousy but about some other matter.

  One day after one of these fights Pete was thinking about how upset he made himself with jealousy. He tried to look at the situation in a more objective way—the way an outside observer would. After a while he was able to say to himself: *"There are things about my wife I find attractive. It is only natural that other men will sometimes find her attractive too. If that happens it does not mean I will lose her. My fears and anger come from doubting my worth. If other men like her, it only confirms what I already know—and that's positive."*

  ✳ Joe's jealousy was even stronger than Pete's. He would question his girlfriend at length when she came home, asking where she had been, who she had been with, and the details of her activities. He sometimes tore himself up wondering if she was having an affair. He would get urges to follow her everywhere or demand that she stay home. It seemed that the more he questioned her the more he disbelieved her.

  It was after hearing his friend talk about wanting to have an affair that Joe realized what was happening. The times when he was most suspicious of his girlfriend were the times when <u>he</u> was having sexual or romantic fantasies about other <u>women</u>. Now when he noticed jealousy, he asked himself: *"Am I just thinking that she's having these fantasies because I'm feeling guilty about my own?"*

For many men, mentioning jealous feelings is not a cool thing to do—to admit jealousy is to admit a weakness. If, however, you view some jealousy as natural and as another OK emotion to share with your partner, both you and your partner can have the privilege of getting to know you better.

  ✳ Karl found that the best way for him to tame the monster was to let his wife know when he felt jealous. He felt very relieved being able to talk about it. Instead of responding with ridicule, his wife seemed to respect him more. Both of them went on to say what behavior of the partner they could and could not tolerate—affairs, flirting, etc. They were able to work out some contracts that specified the limits of the relationship.

What Pete, Joe, and Karl learned about taming jealousy was the following:

1. Some jealousy is normal, and it's best to talk about it rather than hide it.

2. Men can choose to see their partner's attractiveness and behavior as either negative or positive—if they see it negatively, they are likely to upset themselves and waste energy.

3. It will help me to ask: *"Is my jealousy coming from my guilt about my own fantasies or behavior?"*

4. Men have the right to request and contract for some specific limits on their partner's behavior (not thoughts), and women have the same right.

MISINTERPRETATIONS*

Many men who have not been violent think differently about their wives than many men who have.

The main difference has to do with what is called reading negative intent. A man who has been violent is much more likely to think that his wife's or partner's behavior was intended to hurt and humiliate him. He cannot just attribute her behavior to the fact that she is different from him, or that she wasn't thinking, or even that she may have been quite insensitive. He is more likely to think like this:

- *"She was <u>trying</u> to make me angry."*
- *"She was <u>trying</u> to hurt my feelings."*
- *"She was <u>trying</u> to put me down."*
- *"She was <u>trying</u> to get something for herself."*
- *"She was <u>trying</u> to pick a fight."*

And—of course—when a man perceives his wife or partner in this way, he is much more likely to feel justified in responding in an abusive or aggressive fashion.

Other men might think something like this:

- *"I wish she would spend some more time with me here; I'll go over and talk with her."*
- *"She sometimes forgets that I'm not a good mixer; I'll talk to her about what I need the next time we go out."*
- *"I'm glad she's having a good time. She's a very attractive woman."*

Discuss the self-talk <u>about your partner's intentions</u> you might use in the following situations:

- You are at a social gathering and you notice that for the past half-hour your wife has been talking and laughing with the same attractive man. He seems to be flirting with her.
- You are interested in sex and let your girlfriend know this. She isn't very interested, but agrees to have sex. You begin to start things, making romantic moves. After a little while, you notice that she isn't very responsive; she doesn't seem to be very "turned on" or interested in what you are doing.

---

*Adapted with permission from Holtzworth-Munroe & Hutchinson, 1993; the five negative intentions and the two hypothetical situations are directly from that paper. May not be reproduced without permission.

Session 13
PUT-DOWNS

Materials:

> *Weekly Check-in*
> *The Great Santini tape: Scene II*
> *"Put-downs from Parents"*

Goal:

> To help men understand the ways that shaming and put-down messages from their family of origin helped shape their hypersensitivity to shame.

Tasks:

> 1. *Review Weekly Check-in.*
> 2. *Review "Jealousy" homework.*
> 3. *Play Anger Ladder tape and discuss.*
> 4. *Discuss shame research.*
> 5. *Play The Great Santini tape: Scene II*
> 6. *Review "Put-downs from Parents."*
> 7. *Use this information to generate discussion about personal experiences of shame and put-downs.*
> 8. *Review current patterns of shame-based self-talk in relationships.*
> 9. *Explain "Accountability Defenses" and assign as homework.*

Program:

1. Before reviewing the "Put-downs from Parents" homework, the group leaders should present some basic ideas from Dutton's research about the relationship between male shame and domestic violence (see Dutton, D., with Golant, S., 1995; Dutton, van Ginkel, & Strazomski, 1995).

    This research showed that the recollections of assaultive males were characterized by memories of rejecting, cold, and abusive fathers. In analysis after analysis, the scales measuring rejection were more important in influencing future abusiveness than those measuring physical abuse in childhood alone. The research showed that wife assaulters have experienced childhoods characterized by shame, humiliation, embarrassment, and global attacks on their sense of self. Their parents would often publicly humiliate them or punish them at random.

Typical shaming comments include the following:

- *"You're no good."*
- *"You'll never amount to anything."*
- *"I should have had an abortion."*
- *"It's your fault that my life is a mess."*

People who have been exposed to shame will do *anything* to avoid it in the future. They blame others for their behavior. The result is a man who sometimes needs affection but cannot ask for it, is sometimes vulnerable but can't admit it, and is often hurt by some small symbol of lack of love but can only criticize.

When males have been rejected and shamed by their fathers, they become hypersensitive to situations that *might* be interpreted as shame situations in the future. So they are quicker to experience shame, and quicker to feel like they have to *do something* immediately to wipe it out. In these cases, men often blame their wives for making them feel this shame or humiliation, and they turn their rage on their partners to regain some sense of self. If it happens repeatedly with more than one woman, men may go from blaming her to blaming "them."

2. In presenting these ideas, use the word "put-down" rather than "shame" or "humiliation." The word "shame" is likely to lead to defensiveness and denial, and the word "put-down" can be interchanged to present the same ideas.

3. Play *The Great Santini* tape: Scene II (begin at 31:48 and end at 40:23). Discuss the ways in which the father relentlessly attempts to humiliate his son because of his own insecurities. Guide the group discussion with the following questions:

   - How does Ben feel in this situation?
   - Would you want your son to feel like this?
   - What was the Great Santini's <u>intention?</u> Was he trying to humiliate his son? Or was he trying to bring out the highest level of excellence in a way that turned out to be destructive?

4. After this general discussion, review the "Put-downs from Parents" questionnaire from last week's homework. These scales are not to be scored. They are only intended to help stimulate memories and discussion. Ask the men if they can identify experiences similar to Ben's in the movie.

5. Make sure to point out the connection between shame experiences from the past and self-talk in the present, particularly in marital situations. The basic formula to emphasize is that men who were shamed (particularly by their fathers) as boys are especially sensitive to possible shaming situations as adults. So they are likely to tell themselves—more frequently than others—that they are being shamed. And they are likely to feel compelled to take some action to obliterate the perceived source of the shame.

   - Can you identify ways in which you may be hypersensitive to criticism or put-downs because of your experiences as a child?

Homework

1. Complete "Accountability Defenses."

PUT-DOWNS FROM PARENTS*

 **Handout**

Please write in the number listed below (1–4) that best describes how often the experience happened to you with your mother (or stepmother, female guardian, etc.) and father (or stepfather, male guardian, etc.) when you were growing up. If you had more than one mother/father figure, please answer for the persons whom you feel played the most important role in your upbringing.

1	2	3	4
Never Occurred	Occasionally Occurred	Often Occurred	Always Occurred

	Father	**Mother**
1. I think that my parent wished I had been different in some way.	_____	_____
2. As a child, I was physically punished or scolded in the presence of others.	_____	_____
3. My parent would say something about me in front of others so that I felt ashamed.	_____	_____
4. I was treated as the "black sheep" or "scapegoat" of the family.	_____	_____
5. I felt my parent thought it was my fault when he/she was unhappy.	_____	_____
6. I think my parent was mean and held grudges toward me.	_____	_____
7. I was punished by my parents without having done anything.	_____	_____
8. My parent criticized me and/or told me how useless I was in front of others.	_____	_____
9. My parent beat me for no reason.	_____	_____
10. My parent treated me in such a way that I felt ashamed.	_____	_____
11. My parent would be angry with me without letting me know why.	_____	_____

*Adapted with permission from Dutton, van Ginkel, & Strazomski (1995) from the EMBU: Memories of My Upbringing scale. May not be reproduced without permission.

Session 14
ACCOUNTABILITY

Materials:

Weekly Check-in
"Accountability Defenses"
"Accountability Statement"

Goal:

To help the group members gain as clear an understanding as possible of their own destructive behaviors and the rationalizations they have used to justify them.

Tasks:

---

1. Review Weekly Check-In.

2. Review "Accountability Defenses" homework.

3. Review "Accountability Statement" in detail with each group member.

Program:

1. Review "Accountability Defenses" and spend some time discussing individual answers. Make sure that all group members clearly understand each of the defenses and specifically identify some of their own.

2. Introduce the "Accountability Statement." Review each line carefully. Assist the men in filling out their own form using group discussion. In this structured discussion, each group member should be able to identify specific ways in which he has acted destructively in his primary relationship. This is purposely structured so that <u>anyone</u> could identify incidents that would fit this description. We are hoping to create a nondefensive atmosphere in which the men can openly recognize their abusive behaviors and clearly identify the ways in which—at that particular time—they justified them. If you have background information on the incident history, either from the men's previous reports or from previous documentation, it can be helpful to "remind" them of examples of behavior destructive to the relationship. This review is designed to give the men time to examine their behavior and self-talk in some detail and to generate group discussion about the rationalization process. Refer to Commandment 1 (We are all 100% responsible for our own behavior) throughout this discussion.

ACCOUNTABILITY DEFENSES

 **Handout**

Most people who behave destructively toward a partner justify it in their own minds. Even though they do not usually believe in being abusive towards a family member or partner, in certain situations they "make an exception."

Then, afterwards, they figure out some way to make it OK, rather than simply saying the obvious: "I blew it. I crossed over a line, and it's nobody's fault but my own."

Here are some typical examples. Circle any that you have used and write in the specific words that you have said to yourself or others:

- NO BIG DEAL: "I wasn't violent; all I did was slap her."

- INTENTION: "I didn't mean to hurt her—I just wanted her to understand!"

- SELF-EXPRESSION: "It was *my* turn to let her know what I've been going through!"

- DENIAL: "It didn't happen; she's lying!"

- INTOXICATION: "I was drunk; what can I say?"

- LOSS OF CONTROL: "I just flipped out; I didn't even know what I was doing."

- PROJECTION OF BLAME: "It's her fault; if she hadn't pushed me, or nagged me, or spent too much money. . . ."

- DISTORTION OF ROLE: "I had to get physical with her for her own good—she was acting so crazy!"

ACCOUNTABILITY STATEMENT*

 **Handout**

To be accountable means to acknowledge and take responsibility for one's actions. This handout will help you acknowledge destructive behavior in relationships. Although such behavior does not always turn into physical abuse, practically everyone—in almost <u>all</u> emotionally intimate relationships—behaves abusively at times. This is an opportunity to assess ways in which you recognize past mistakes and can demonstrate a desire to change them. As you fill out this form, remember Commandment 1: "We are all 100% responsible for our own actions." You will not be turning this in, but we will use what you have written in our group discussion. We are not asking you to admit to something that you did not do or to take responsibility for something that someone else has done.

- I have acted in the following destructive ways toward my partner. (Circle each):

Verbal abuse:	Put-downs	Isolation of partner	Controlling partner
Manipulation of children	Stalking	Economic abuse	Intimidation
Threats Monitoring mail/phone		Ignoring	Mind-games
Sexual abuse: Forced sex acts	Sexual humiliation		Demanding sex
Sexual put downs			
Physical abuse: Physical restraint	Pushing	Slapping	Kicking
Punching Throwing things	Property destruction Choking		Use of weapons

Other_____

- I take responsibility for these destructive behaviors. My behavior was not <u>caused</u> by my partner. I had a choice.
- I have used the following to rationalize my destructive behaviors in this relationship (e.g., alcohol, stress, anger, "she was nagging me," etc.)

1. _____

2. _____

3. _____

- I recognize that my partner may be distrustful, intimidated, and fearful of me because of these behaviors.

---

*Adapted with permission from Pence, E., & Paymar, M. 1993. May not be reproduced without permission.

Session 15
SWITCH!

Materials:

Weekly Check-in
"Dangerous Self-talk"
"Confident Self-talk"
"Switch!"

Goal:

To rehearse and integrate all of the skills learned in the self-management section.

Tasks:

> *1. Review Weekly Check-in.*
> *2. Review "Dangerous Self-talk."*
> *3. Review "Confident Self-talk."*
> *4. Practice "Switch!" with half of the group members.*

Program:

1. Review "Dangerous Self-talk" and "Confident Self-talk." This is designed to reinforce the self-talk themes and to prepare the men for the "Switch!" exercise.

2. Ask a volunteer to pick a stressful situation to practice new skills. Lead the men through the steps of "Switch!" This is a very important opportunity to assess how well the group members are able to examine themselves and integrate new ideas. General instructions should be given, such as: *"When role-playing this situation, combine all the skills you've learned so far: use relaxation skills, build up your self-esteem, challenge your 'bad rap,' and think constructively."*

   - The first two steps of "Switch!" are used to **identify the problem situation and identify the self-talk.** The target member describes the thoughts he was having before, during, and after the problem situation.
   - The next step, **determining new self-talk,** focuses on what the person would like to develop as coping self-talk. The group members should help generate "counter" self-talk.

112

- In **modeling the situation,** the leader demonstrates the process of switching from self-defeating to self-enhancing statements, which the target member will practice during "Switch!"

- Now the reframing begins. The target member is asked to **imagine that he is back in the problem situation.** The leader further instructs the target member to begin stating aloud the self-defeating self-talk. When the group leader gives the command, the group—in very loud unison—yells "**SWITCH!**" and the target member inserts the new self-talk.

   Note: This is meant to be entertaining—and to provide a shock to the individual's typical self-talk patterns!

- Both **self-evaluation** and **group feedback** follow. Group members should give feedback initially on aspects of the self-talk reframing that were done well, followed by suggestions for improvement.

3. Practice the "Switch!" exercise with half of the group members. Ask them to choose a disturbing situation from the past—perhaps *"the incident that got you here."* All group members should go through this exercise over the next two sessions. Remember that you are trying to assess their ability to examine personal responsibility—and new options—for abusive behavior.

DANGEROUS SELF-TALK*

Handout

* She wants to be with someone else.
* She's trying to humiliate me.
* Here we go again!
* I never get my way.
* No one understands.
* No one gets away with that with me.
* If I'm not tough she'll think I'm weak.
* I need to show her I'm in control.
* If she talks to another man it means she wants to go to bed with him.
* She does nothing but stay home and take care of the kids and talk on the phone.
* If other men look at her it means she is flirting with them and that demeans me.
* The kids don't respect me because of her.
* She's out to make me a fool.
* When she wants time for herself, it means she doesn't want me.
* When she's not there when I want her, it means she doesn't care.
* I'm sick and tired of all this crap.
* No matter what I do it won't be good enough.
* When she doesn't want sex, it means she doesn't really care or she's cheating on me.
* The kids are more important to her than I am.
* Her friends are more important to her than I am.
* Her family is more important to her than I am.

---

*Adapted with permission from Michael Lindsey, Ph.D. May not be reproduced without permission.

CONFIDENT SELF-TALK*

 **Handout**

* These thoughts will get me nowhere.
* I trust her.
* She hasn't given me any reason not to trust her.
* She may be right.
* I can be assertive.
* I can take a time-out.
* I'm important to her even though it may not seem that way now.
* I'm in control of my own reactions.
* She can't get me upset unless I allow her to.
* It's too nice of a day to get upset.
* I need to do something for myself that's relaxing.
* It's okay that she's angry; I don't have to settle it right now.
* I can say no.
* I can negotiate and offer a compromise.
* I can ask for what I want.

SWITCH!

Handout

1. *What went wrong?*
   a. Who was involved? When was it? Where was it? Describe exactly what was happening. Be specific and objective.

   b. Replay this like a movie. What exactly did you do and say?

   c. Other group members should help by asking questions so the "movie" is very clear.

2. *What was my self-talk?*
   a. What was your self-talk before, during, and after the situation?

   b. Freeze the frame of this movie so you can stop at different points and identify the self-talk.

   c. With the group's help, analyze the self-defeating or unproductive self-talk.

3. *What new, more productive self-talk could I have used?*
   a. What would you like to have said to yourself instead in this situation?

   b. Brainstorm with group for alternative self-talk.

4. *Self-talk "Switch."*
   a. Put yourself back in the problem situation.

   b. Practice the old self-talk out loud.

   c. When the group calls out **"Switch!,"** try using your productive self-talk instead.

5. *What do you think? What does the group think?*
   a. Did you use any self-defeating self-talk that you did not correct?

   b. Did you switch effectively from self-defeating to more productive self-talk?

Session 16
SKILLS INTEGRATION

Materials:

Weekly Check-in
"Joe's Self-talk"
"Switch!" (from Session 15)

Goal:

To rehearse and integrate all of the skills learned in the self-management section.

Tasks:

1. *Review Weekly Check-in.*
2. *Review "Joe's Self-talk."*
3. *Practice "Switch!" with half of the group members.*

Program:

1. Review "Joe's Self-talk" handout. Use discussion around this handout to offer the men more information about how the "bad rap" can generate destructive actions.

2. Ask a volunteer to pick a stressful situation to practice new skills. Lead the men through the steps of "Switch!" (as outlined on p. 116).

JOE'S SELF-TALK*

Handout

"I'm Joe. Last July my wife and I got into an argument over money problems. It seems like we're always at each other about bills. She never shows me any respect. Anyway, she was bitching about the fact that we didn't have any money and that we were always broke. She kept arguing and yelling until I couldn't take it anymore, so I told her that she had better shut up. She kept on yelling, so I grabbed her and told her to shut up or else. The next day I got a court order and the judge says that I have to go to counseling and these meetings, so here I am. Sometimes I fly off the handle when she gets me going, but I don't really get violent. I mean I don't think I'm a batterer or anything. I slapped her a couple times when I had been drinking, but only when I was drinking."

So here's the sequence of Joe's self-talk and internal logic:

1. *She was arguing and yelling*

2. *So I should tell her to shut up*

3. *She keeps on hassling me*

4. *So I should grab her and threaten her*

Joe's story tells us a lot about his self-talk. Here is some of the self-talk that probably leads him to these attitudes and behaviors:

- *I have the right to make her shut up when she is saying things that I don't want to hear.*
- *If I tell her to stop doing something and she keeps doing it, I can physically stop her.*
- *If I tell her to do something once or twice or even more and she doesn't do it, she is pushing me to hit her.*
- *It is partially her fault that I hit her.*
- *I had no other choices that were acceptable to me.*

What do you think? Do you recognize some of this self-talk in yourself? Can you see how this self-talk sets the stage for aggressive or abusive behavior?

---

*Adapted with permission from Pence & Paymar, 1993. May not be reproduced without permission.

RELATIONSHIP SKILLS

Session 17
ASSERTIVENESS

Materials:

> *Weekly Check-in*
> *"Assertiveness"*
> *"What Is Assertive Behavior?"*
> *"Keeping Track"*

Goal:

> To teach the men to be more assertive through self-awareness and cognitive restructuring.

Tasks:

> 1. *Review Weekly Check-in.*
> 2. *Review "Assertiveness."*
> 3. *Discuss the four types of behavior.*
> 4. *Discuss "What Is Assertive Behavior?"*
> 5. *Model and role play assertive behavior.*
> 6. *Assign homework.*

Program:

> Review "Assertiveness" and "What Is Assertive Behavior?" as a way of giving basic education about assertiveness and of getting the men to become aware of their own degree of assertiveness. While discussing the four types of behaviors in the first handout, encourage the men to give examples. The group leaders should give other examples, then model and role play the different assertive behaviors. Encourage the men to think of benefits of assertiveness for them personally or to the relationship.
>
> Remind the group members that these are tools, not rules. Sometimes it makes sense to be passive, and sometimes (like in self-defense situations) it even makes sense to be aggressive. These tools are all designed primarily for relationships that we <u>care</u> about—relationships that we want to preserve as respectfully as possible.

121

Homework

1. Use the "Keeping Track" handout to describe a situation that upset you and what you might have done differently.

ASSERTIVENESS

Handout

1. **Assertive.** This behavior involves knowing what you feel and want. It also involves expressing your feelings and needs directly and honestly without violating the rights of others. At all times you are accepting responsibility for your feelings and actions.

   "It bothered me when you were late coming back from shopping, because I had to rush off to work."

2. **Aggressive.** This type of behavior involves attacking someone else, being controlling, provoking, and maybe even violent. Its consequences could be destructive to others as well as yourself.

   "What the hell's wrong with you? All you ever think about is yourself!"

3. **Passive.** The person withdraws, becomes anxious, and avoids confrontation. Passive people let others think for them, make decisions for them and tell them what to do.

   He feels resentful but doesn't express it or deal with it. He feels like it's useless: either he doesn't deserve any better, or nobody will ever listen to him anyway. Usually he will become depressed, and he may believe that his wife or partner is purposely trying to take advantage of him—but he does nothing about the situation.

4. **Passive-aggressive.** In this behavior the person is not direct in relating to people, does not accept what is happening—but will retaliate in an indirect manner. This type of behavior can cause confusion. The other person feels "stung," but can't be exactly sure how or why. And the person who has done the stinging can act like he has done nothing at all—and imply that the other person is just "too sensitive."

   The man acts cold to his girlfriend, then pretends like nothing's wrong when she asks him about it.

   Or a man who is feeling unappreciated by his wife "forgets" to give her a phone message. Or makes some "joking" comment about her weight!

WHAT IS ASSERTIVE BEHAVIOR?*

 **Handout**

1. Asking for what you want but not being demanding.

2. Expressing feelings.

3. Genuinely expressing feedback or compliments to others and accepting them.

4. Disagreeing, without being aggressive.

5. Asking questions and getting information from others.

6. Using "I" messages and "I feel" statements without being judgmental or blaming.

7. Making eye contact during a conversation (unless this is inappropriate in the person's culture).

EXAMPLES:

1. "Can you give me some feedback about how I handled the kids' homework tonight?"

2. "I feel embarrassed when you tease me about my weight in front of my friends."

3. "Mom, I know you want us to call more often, but I don't think you realize how busy we both are."

4. "Corey, I just saw your report card and I'm concerned. Let's sit down and talk about this together."

5. "Sarah, I'd like to talk about this later after we've both cooled off."

6. Look the person in the eye and say, "I really care about you, let's work this out."

KEEPING TRACK

 **Handout**

Keep a record of a situation that upset you during the week. Record the information below. As you think about it, record what would have been the best response in this situation.

Situation & Date	
Physical Cues (my own)	
Self-Talk	
How I Felt	
My Behavior	
Best Response	

Session 18

EXPRESSING FEELINGS AND ASKING FOR CHANGE

Materials:

Weekly Check-in
"Requests & Refusals"
"'I' Messages or Asking for Change"
"Keeping Track" (from Session 17)

Goal:

To teach the men specific techniques to express feelings and request change from others.

Tasks:

1. *Review Weekly Check-In.*
2. *Review homework.*
3. *Review and practice "Requests & Refusals."*
4. *Review and practice "'I' Messages or Asking for Change."*
5. *Assign homework.*

Program:

Explain the concept of assertive requests from the handout, "Requests & Refusals." Make it clear that these requests are presented as questions, not as statements or demands. Discuss the two types of assertive requests.

2. Model and role-play assertive requests for each of the situations and discuss.

3. Explain the concept of assertive refusals from the handout, "Requests & Refusals."

4. Model and role-play assertive refusal for each of the situations and discuss.

Homework

1. Fill out "What Can You Ask?" Practice the different skills you learned in the session today. Write down why some of the requests were more difficult than others.

2. Describe a situation that upset you during the week in the "Keeping Track" handout. As you think about it, record what you would <u>like</u> to have done in this situation.

REQUESTS & REFUSALS

 **Handout**

Assertive Requests: These are presented as questions, not as statements or demands. There are two types of assertive requests:

- Requests for behavior from another person. This request is used when you would like someone to start doing something that you like—or stop doing something that you don't like.
- Requests for verbal responses from someone else. This type is used when you would like information from someone. It is especially useful when you think that someone is pressuring you and you want clarification.

Try using assertive requests for the following scenes:

- Ask to borrow money from a friend.
- Ask someone in a waiting room to stop smoking because it is bothering your child.
- Ask the lawyer you hired (whom you haven't heard from in a month) to speed up your case.
- Ask a teacher or a supervisor for a letter of recommendation.

Assertive Refusal: These are presented in a clear, respectful way. Here are some guidelines:

- Clearly state "No."
- Offer a reason for the "No." (not always needed)
- Suggest an alternative for how the other person can get his or her needs met.
- Consider offering to help—but at some other time or under other conditions.

Try using assertive refusals for the following scenes:

- "Excuse me—could I borrow your car today?"
- "Am I glad I found you—I really need to borrow $20!"
- "I want to talk about this <u>right now</u>!"
- "We're all going out for a drink after work. You used to love to party! Come on and join us—one drink won't hurt you!"

"I" MESSAGES OR ASKING FOR CHANGE

One method to use when you want to communicate your feelings, meanings, and intentions is "I" messages. "I" messages are specific, nonjudgmental, and focus on you. In contrast, "you" messages are hostile, blaming, and focused on the other person. Reframing "you" messages into "I" messages can help you communicate—because the other person will not feel attacked.

TO CONSTRUCT AN "I" MESSAGE:

1. Describe the behavior that is affecting you (just describe, don't blame).

2. Explain your feeling about how the behavior affects you.

You may want to go on to Steps 3 & 4.

3. Specify a new behavior that you would like the other person to use instead.

4. Offer a positive consequence in exchange.

CONSTRUCT "I" MESSAGES BY USING THESE PHRASES:

1. When you (state the behavior).

2. I feel (state the feeling) **because** (explain in more detail).

Note: Using the word *because* with an explanation can help by giving the other person more information to understand you.

You may want to go on to Steps 3 & 4.

3. I wish (state what you would prefer instead).

4. And if you can do that, I will (explain how the other person will benefit).

The different parts of the "I" message do not have to be delivered in exact order. The important thing is to keep the focus on yourself and to stay away from blame.

- When you take long phone calls during dinner, I get angry because I begin to think you don't want to talk to me.
- I wish you would tell whoever's calling that you'll call back because we're in the middle of dinner.
- And if you can do that, I'll make sure not to hassle you so much about being on the phone later.

- When you don't come home or call, I get worried that something has happened to you.
- I would really like you to call me if you're going to be late.
- And if you can do that, I promise not to have an attitude when you get home.

- When you yell at me right in the middle of a busy time at work, I get so rattled that I end up making more mistakes.
- I wish that you would lighten up when you know that I'm busy.
- And if you can do that, I will be a lot easier to work with.

Session 19
HANDLING CRITICISM

Materials:

Weekly Check-in
"Handling Criticism"
"Keeping Track" (from Session 17)

Goal:

To teach the group members specific ways of dealing with criticism effectively.

Tasks:

1. *Review Weekly Check-in.*
2. *Review homework.*
3. *Review the handout "Handling Criticism."*
4. *Model assertive responses to criticism.*
5. *Guide group members through role-play of handling criticism.*
6. *Assign homework.*

Program:

1. Usually spouses are critical of each other—constructively or destructively. It is difficult for most people to deal with criticism, and in most cases they get defensive. A major part of communicating effectively is learning to give constructive criticism as well as to receive criticism. Therefore, the objective of this session is to teach skills in taking criticism.

   Give the group members the handout, "Handling Criticism." The nonconstructive ways of dealing with criticism can be portrayed in a humorous way. Use examples and role-play when teaching the constructive ways of handling criticism.

2. Pay particular attention to the attitudes men have about women's anger. Discuss how men "trivialize" women's anger:
   - *"She's on the rag."*
   - *"You're so cute when you're angry."*
   - Laughing at her when she is upset.

Homework

1. Write down two examples of situations when you thought that your wife or partner was being critical. Write your feelings and whether the criticism was constructive or destructive. Describe exactly how you handled it: your self-talk, your feelings, and your response. Discuss how you might have handled it better.

   ✳ *Criticism:*

      Self-Talk:

      Feelings:

      Your Response:

      Better Response?:

2. Describe a situation that upset you during the week in the "Keeping Track" handout. As you think about it, record what you would <u>like</u> to have done in this situation.

HANDLING CRITICISM*

Handout

A. DESTRUCTIVE RESPONSES

Everyone is occasionally criticized. How you handle criticism is especially important in intimate relationships. It is not uncommon to react defensively. Typical responses to criticism are the following:

1. *Avoid the criticism or critic.* Ignore, change the subject, make jokes (be funny), refuse to talk about it, be too busy, withdraw, or even walk away.

   - When someone says something critical to you, don't respond verbally, just fire them a "go to hell" look, and walk out of the room.
   - When the other person is talking to you, look at the floor, stare into space, or just look through them. Avoid making direct eye contact.
   - *"I don't want to talk about this—subject closed!"*
   - Suppose you are late for work and your boss confronts you. You could change the subject by talking about getting your car fixed so <u>it</u> will be more reliable.

Practice "avoiding": Your wife says to you, *"You don't help much with the housework around here."* What do you do?

2. *Deny the critical comment.* Deny facts, argue, present evidence, do not take any responsibility for anything.

   - Argue about the facts. Fight about all the minor details. For example, *"No, I didn't call your mother a toad, I said she was always croaking about something."*
   - Deny that it happened. *"I wasn't drunk at the party."*
   - *"I don't know what you're talking about, I don't understand."*

Practice "denying": Your wife or partner has made dinner for both of you. After you come home an hour late from playing basketball, she says, *"I don't know why I bother to treat you well. You should have been home when you told me you would be!"* What do you do?

---

*Adapted from Geffner & Mantooth, 1995. May not be reproduced without permission.

3. ***Make excuses.*** Explain your behavior in detail, be very sorry, have an alibi or excuse, or argue the importance of your behavior.

- You were late to pick up your girlfriend, so you go into detail about how the keys got lost, you had to search for them, and the baby is always losing everything. Your girlfriend will soon just want to forget she ever said anything.

- Again you are late and your girlfriend is upset. Make statements like, *"Well, it was just a movie, look at all the important things I have to take care of every day."*

- *"So I had my tongue in her ear at the party, that doesn't mean I care about her. You know you're the only one for me."*

Practice *"excuses"*: You are getting phone calls from an old girlfriend and not doing anything to discourage them. Your wife says, *"You obviously care a lot more about her than you do about me. You tell her to stop calling this house!"* What do you do?

4. ***Fight back.*** Attack, get even, the best defense is a good offense, fight fire with fire. This can be aggressive or passive-aggressive.

- Suppose a family member says something about your gaining some weight. Attack his or her weight, housekeeping, handwriting, etc.

- You could get even by being careless with his furniture and spilling something, or being late when she really wanted to be somewhere on time.

- *"Why do you always bring these things up at the wrong time? Don't you know how stressed out I am?"*

- *"Why are you always such a bitch?"*

- Grab your wife, put your hand over her mouth, threaten to hit her if she doesn't shut up.

Practice "fighting back": You drove home after having too many beers. Your wife says, *"That was so stupid. Don't you even care about me or the kids?"* What do you do?

B. CONSTRUCTIVE RESPONSES

As you can see, all these ways of handling criticism can seriously hurt good communication and destroy relationships. Major arguments may develop because someone has been ignored, argued with, or attacked. Since the common responses to criticism are so destructive to communication and relationships, try these instead:

1. ***Ask for details.*** Criticisms are often vague or given in generalities. For example, "You're lazy" or "I don't like the way you're acting." When you ask for details you find out exactly what the other person is talking about.

- *"Can you please tell me more?"*

- *"Would you please be more specific so I can understand?"*

- Suggest possible complaints and ask whether these might be the problem. *"Are you upset because I didn't pay enough attention to you at the party?"*

- Your wife or partner says, *"You're rude."* Respond, *"Yeah, sometimes I can be rude. I know that. But what have I done just now that sounds rude to you?"*

2. *Agree with the accurate part of the criticism.* A second step to handling criticism effectively is to agree with the part of the criticism that is true.

   - Suppose you go to a movie and you liked the movie but your girlfriend criticizes you for liking it. Instead of getting defensive, say *"Yeah, I like these adventure movies; I guess we have different taste in movies."*

   - Agree in principle. *"Yes, it would be good for my health if I gave up smoking, but I'm choosing not to."*

3. *IF SHE IS RIGHT, APOLOGIZE!* This is the most mature and adult thing to do. There is no shame in acknowledging mistakes, as long as it is accompanied by a genuine effort to correct them.

GENERAL GUIDELINES FOR HANDLING CRITICISM:

1. Learn to see criticism as an opportunity to learn and grow.

2. Try to avoid being defensive.

3. Listen actively.

4. Watch nonverbal language.

5. Monitor physical and emotional cues.

6. Act, do not react.

Practice "constructive responses" to the same four situations:

1. Your wife says to you, *"I really need some more help with the housework around here."* What do you do?

2. Your wife or partner has made dinner for both of you. After you come home an hour late from playing basketball, she says, *"I don't know why I bother to treat you well. You should have been home when you told me you would be!"* What do you do?

3. You are getting phone calls from an old girlfriend and not doing anything to discourage them. Your wife says, *"I don't like this. You tell her to stop calling this house!"* What do you do?

4. You drove home after having too many beers. Your wife says, *"That was so stupid. Don't you even care about me or the kids?"* What do you do?

Session 20
EXPRESSING FEELINGS AND ACTIVE LISTENING

Materials:

> *Weekly Check-in*
> *The Great Santini tape: Scene III*
> *"Expressing Your Feelings"*
> *"Active Listening"*

Goal:

> To learn to express feelings and to listen to the feelings of others.

Tasks:

> 1. *Review Weekly Check-in.*
> 2. *Review homework.*
> 3. *Play The Great Santini: Scene III and discuss.*
> 4. *Review "Expressing Your Feelings." Role-play and discuss.*
> 5. *Review "Active Listening."*
> 6. *Model and role-play active listening examples.*
> 7. *Assign homework.*

Program:

1. Play The Great Santini: Scene III and discuss (thanks to James A. Reavis, Psy.D. for these discussion guidelines).
   a. Discuss the Great Santini's genuine desire to emotionally connect with his son, as well as his absolute inability to do so. This is a man who is simply unable to identify or express his own emotions.
   b. Compare his effort with that of his wife, who is perfectly able to tell her son how much she loves him. From her, Ben <u>knows</u> that he is loved, he develops the potential to connect with others in this way, and he develops emotional confidence and self-assurance.
   c. Discuss the ways in which group members were exposed to different styles of emotional communication. Remember Dutton's research (see Dutton, D., with Golant, S. 1995) on domestic violence offenders and their rela-

tionships with their fathers: filled with shameful episodes and emotional distance.

   d. Ask the group members what models for emotional expression they want to offer their sons.

2. Review the "Expressing Your Feelings" handout. Role-play the different situations. Review assertive and non-assertive ways of expressing feelings in these situations. Discuss the different ways we decide whether or not a situation is worth a response.

3. Review the "Active Listening" handout. Explain the basic concepts, then model and role-play active listening based on the different examples.

Homework

1. Record three examples of your "Active Listening" responses over the next week.

   * Situation:

     You Said:

   * Situation:

     You Said:

   * Situation:

     You Said:

EXPRESSING YOUR FEELINGS

 **Handout**

For each situation below:

- **Identify your feelings.**
- **Put into words how you might express your feelings. Remember to use "I feel" statements.**
- **Remember that you don't always have to respond. If you would choose to say nothing in any of these situations, describe your feelings.**

1. Your girlfriend was going to meet you downtown for lunch, and you have been waiting over an hour. She finally arrives and says she had a few errands to run before she came.

2. A friend of yours makes a "joking" comment about how your wife is "a little on the hefty side."

3. Your wife teases you in front of your friends about how much trouble you have trying to fix things around the house.

4. You are late getting home and your wife or partner demands an explanation, but as soon as you begin she interrupts and starts yelling and saying how inconsiderate you are.

ACTIVE LISTENING

 Handout

Active listening is a communication technique that encourages the other person to continue speaking. It also enables you to be certain you understand what the other person is saying. It's a way of checking it out. It's called *active* listening because you not only listen but also *actively* let the other person know that you have really heard her.

A. ACTIVE LISTENING INVOLVES PARAPHRASING.

1. *Paraphrasing* is stating in your own words what you think the other person has said.
- *"You sound really (feeling)   about (situation) ."*
- *"You must really feel (feeling)   ."*
- *"What I hear you saying is_____ ."*

B. ACTIVE LISTENING ALSO INVOLVES CLARIFYING.

1. *Clarifying* involves asking questions to get more information.

2. *Clarifying* helps you hear more specifics about the situation and feelings.

3. *Clarifying* also lets the other person know you are interested in what he or she is saying.
- *"So, tell me what happened that got you so upset."*
- *"How did you feel when that happened?"*

C. ACTIVE LISTENING OFTEN INVOLVES PERSONALIZING.

1. *Personalizing* involves offering a personal example of feeling the same thing or being in the same situation.
- *"I think I know what you mean. I've been there too."*
- *"I felt the same way when I lost my job. I think everyone does."*

2. *Personalizing* helps the other person feel less alone, and it implies that someone else has experienced this and recovered from it.

3. *Personalizing* can be harmful if you talk <u>too</u> much about yourself and steal the spotlight from the person who needs it.
- *"You think that was bad? Listen to what happened to me!"*

D. ACTIVE LISTENING DOES <u>NOT</u> MEAN CHEERING UP, DEFENDING YOURSELF, JUDGING THE PERSON, OR JUST REPEATING BACK EXACTLY WHAT WAS SAID.

- All I ever do is the dirty work around here!
  "Oh, come on, it's a hot day, you're just in a bad mood, don't worry about it."

- You can't trust anyone around this place!

  "Now, now, it's OK. It's all going to be better—I'll take care of it for you."
- I'm really worried that my family is going to be mad at me for dropping out of school.

  "You shouldn't feel that way."
- I keep trying to talk to you about how to handle the kids and you never listen to me!

  "I'm in charge! No more discussion!"
- This place is really disgusting.

  "It sounds like you think this place is really disgusting."

Some keys to being a good active listener: Good eye contact, lean slightly forward, reinforce by nodding or paraphrasing, clarify by asking questions, avoid distractions, try to really understand what was said.

Session 21

EMPATHY TRAINING: WHAT MY PARTNER FEELS

Materials:

> *Weekly Check-in*

Goal:

> To help the group members gain as clear an understanding as possible of what the other person is experiencing during a fight or abusive situation.

Tasks:

> 1. *Review Weekly Check-in.*
> 2. *Review homework.*
> 3. *Introduce importance of empathy.*
> 4. *Guide group member through "Empathy Training" exercise.*
> 5. *Review with group member what he has learned from this exercise.*
> 6. *Continue with several more group members.*

Program:

1. Many of the men in our groups lack empathy. Their behavior might be quite different if they were genuinely aware of the effect of their behavior on the other people around them. You might consider saying something like this as an introduction to this session: *You are here because, at some point in the past, you were abusive. At the time, you simply may not have been aware of how you were affecting your wife or partner, or what it must have been like to be in her position. We'd like to help you gain more of that knowledge, so that the next time around you'll be better informed. If you knew then what you know now (or what you are now learning), you might have made other choices.*

2. The instructions are quite simple. A group member describes an interpersonal conflict situation. He is then assigned to take on the role of his partner. Tell the group members to imagine that they are playing the role of their wife or partner:

   This is the "Wives and Partners" group. We have invited you all here today to hear your side of the story. We've heard a lot about what's happened in your family from

141

your husband's or partner's point of view. Now we'd like to hear exactly how you felt and what you went through.

The conflict scene is role played. The volunteer must describe exactly what his wife or partner (for example) is thinking or feeling—without sarcasm, without editorial comments, without trying to make her look bad. The group should keep giving feedback until they think he has played the role just right and has **truly gotten inside the other person's shoes.**

The goal here is not problem-solving, but rather understanding. It is also important to remind the men that gaining an empathic point of view does not necessarily mean agreeing with the other person, but simply understanding what it must feel like to be that person.

3. One way to structure this exercise is to make notes on the board during the check-in process. These notes describe the wife's or partner's point of view in the argument. Then use these for the empathy training exercise. For example:

   - Carrie is suspicious because another woman has been calling me.
   - Denise gets on my case about going off to play basketball.
   - Nina insisted on watching her TV show even though she knew it was time for ESPN SportsCenter.

4. Continue this exercise with as many people as possible. Encourage all the group members to join in with questions and discussion of their fellow "wives and partners."

Session 22
THE FOUR HORSEMEN OF THE APOCALYPSE

Materials:

> *Weekly Check-in*
> *"The Four Horsemen of the Apocalypse"*
> *"Darren and Karen"*
> *"Repair Mechanisms"*

Goals:

> To teach the men about destructive patterns in marital communication; to help them identify these patterns and recognize the negative self-talk that accompanies them.

Tasks:

> 1. *Review Weekly Check-in.*
> 2. *Read and review "The Four Horsemen of the Apocalypse."*
> 3. *Read and role play "Darren and Karen" with group members.*
> 4. *Encourage discussion about self-talk in these communications.*
> 5. *Review "Repair Mechanisms" and role-play alternatives.*
> 6. *Assign homework.*

Program:

> Research by John Gottman and his colleagues (Gottman, 1994) has helped us understand patterns in marital communication that are almost sure to doom a marriage. The handout explains the basic principles and examples of these communication patterns. Use these handouts as a discussion guide for understanding how this works. Ask the men to identify themselves and their partners in these examples.
>
> Make sure to (1) identify the self-talk patterns that govern these patterns, and (2) role play alternatives for how to use different self-talk and different communications.

Homework

1. Identify four situations when you used one of the "repair mechanisms" in communicating with your wife or partner or someone else. Describe the situation and what you said.

   * Situation:

     You Said:

   * Situation:

     You Said:

   * Situation:

     You Said:

   * Situation:

     You Said:

THE FOUR HORSEMEN OF THE APOCALYPSE*

 **Handout**

Fred: *Did you pick up the dry cleaning?*

Ingrid: (In a mocking tone) *"Did you pick up my dry cleaning?"* Pick up your own damn dry cleaning. *What am I, your maid?*

Fred: *Hardly. If you were a maid, at least you'd know how to clean.*

Recent research about marriages has uncovered the Four Horsemen of the Apocalypse: Accusations (Criticism), Defensiveness, Contempt, and Stonewalling. When couples engage in these behaviors frequently, they are much more likely to be volatile. The researchers have found that couples who regularly use these styles with each other are almost certainly headed for unhappiness, verbal or physical abuse, and divorce.

ACCUSATION (CRITICISM): Complaints are expressed in a destructive manner, as an attack on the spouse's character.

When her husband is late and apologizes, Pamela says to him in front of their daughter, "That's OK—it gave us a chance to discuss your amazing ability to screw up every single plan we make. You're so thoughtless and self-centered!"

The differences between complaints and personal accusations are simple. In a complaint, a wife states specifically what is upsetting her, and criticizes her husband's action, not her husband himself, saying how it made her feel.

"When you forget to pick up my clothes at the cleaners, I feel like you don't care about me."

The harsh accusation leaves the person on the receiving end feeling ashamed, disliked, blamed, and defective—all of which are more likely to lead to defensive response than to steps to improve things.

DEFENSIVENESS: Defensiveness is the fighting back response. Here the husband or wife refuses to take in anything the spouse is saying. It is one arm of the typical "fight-or-flight" response: with defensiveness, the individual only knows how to fight.

Defensive husbands are like baseball batters practicing with an automatic pitching machine—and each ball is some sort of criticism or complaint from their wives. They respond this way even with "low-level" complaining, like worry, sadness, or whining. They smash it back, put her down in return, never take any responsibility for what she is saying. They show no interest in what she may be feeling. Defensive husbands never say, "Maybe you're right," or "I see your point," or "I never thought of that," or "Yeah, I get it," or "I think I owe you an apology."

Some nondefensive husbands are effective in maintaining good communication just by listening patiently, or even changing the topic. Sometimes it just means asking questions, using friendly (not sarcastic) humor to defuse the situation, or even gossiping about someone else. One way or another, these nondefensive husbands find a way not to escalate the tension by trying to smash a home run. They are communicating *respect*.

A special type of defensive technique is known as *gaslighting*. Here one partner continues to insist that he or she could never have done what was alleged: "You must have imagined that!" For example: A man slaps his wife or partner in front of a neighbor, then denies it, telling her that this was something he would never do and that

---

*Adapted with permission from Gottman, 1994. May not be reproduced without permission.

something must be wrong with her mind. His neighbor, who was watching the incident, goes along with the story and says that it never happened. Although her face is still red from the slap, she wonders if maybe she just made it up.

CONTEMPT: Contempt is usually expressed not just in the words themselves, but also in a tone of voice and an angry expression—rolling the eyes; a look of disgust.

Research indicates that if a husband shows contempt regularly, his wife will be more prone to a range of health problems, from frequent colds and flus to bladder and yeast infections, as well as gastrointestinal complaints. And when a wife's face shows disgust towards her husband four or more times within a 15-minute conversation, it is a silent sign that the couple is likely to separate within four years.

Habitual criticism and contempt (or disgust) are danger signs because they indicate that a husband or wife has made a silent judgment for the worse about their partner. In his or her thoughts, the spouse is always being condemned.

STONEWALLING: Stonewalling is the ultimate defense. The stonewaller just goes blank and withdraws from the conversation. This sends a powerful message: icy distance, superiority, and distaste. When partners stonewall regularly, it cuts off all possibilities of working out disagreements. Don't confuse stonewalling with time-out. Time-out communicates *respect*. The message is that the husband or wife cares enough about the relationship to make a special effort not to cause any further damage. And there is a very clear contract that the discussion <u>will</u> continue at a future time.

DARREN AND KAREN*

 **Handout**

The children are getting pretty wild, and Darren, their father, is getting annoyed. He turns to his wife, Karen, and says in a sharp tone: *"Dear, don't you think the kids could quiet down?"*

His self-talk *"She's too easy on the kids."*

Karen, responding to his irritation, feels a surge of anger. Her face becomes tense. She answers, *"The kids are having a good time. Anyhow, they'll be going up to bed soon."*

Her self-talk: *"There he goes again, complaining all the time."*

Darren is now visibly enraged. He leans forward menacingly, his fists clenched, as he says in an annoyed tone, *"Should I put them to bed now?"*

His self-talk: *"She opposes me in everything. I'd better take over."*

Karen, suddenly frightened by Darren, says meekly, *"No, I'll put them to bed right away."*

Her self-talk: *"He's getting out of control—he could hurt the kids. I'd better give in."*

WHAT DOES THIS MEAN

For Karen, the background self-talk to this conversation goes like this, *"He's always bullying me with his anger."*

For Darren, the background self-talk goes something like this, *"She has no right to treat me like this!"*

Karen feels like an innocent victim in their marriage, and Darren feels insulted and outraged by what he feels is unjust treatment.

Once these beliefs take root, the are difficult to shake. Both husband and wife will look for any evidence to confirm their point of view. And they forget, or pay less attention to, the positive. Even neutral comments make them both say, *"There he (or she) goes again!"*

---

*Adapted with permission from Gottman, 1994. May not be reproduced without permission.

REPAIR MECHANISMS*

 **Handout**

What can you do differently to keep a conflict from escalating?

Here are some specific things to say when the marital conversation starts to become aggressive, accusatory, contemptuous, avoidant, cold, or defensive. These can help put the conversation back on the track of *mutual respect*.

Remember that tone of voice and body language have as much impact as words. Some of these statements can come across as critical or challenging depending on how they are presented.

- *"Please let me finish."*
- *"We're getting off the topic—I really want us to work this out."*
- *"I'm not mad about this, but that did hurt my feelings."*
- *"Yes. I see what you mean."*
- *"Uh huh, go on."*
- *"I think we're getting off the subject."*
- *"I think I know how you feel. I want you to know you're not alone in feeling that way."*
- *"I like your idea."*
- *"I understand how you feel."*
- *"You know, you're right that I haven't always been involved enough with the kids. Now let's get back to what happened today with you and me."*
- *"I'm really glad you were able to bring this up."*
- *"I'm sorry about that—I had no idea it affected you like that."*
- *"I can understand that you'd be mad about me being late, but let me tell you more about what happened and maybe you'll understand."*

*Adapted with permission from Gottman, 1994. May not be reproduced without permission.

Session 23

COMPLIMENTS: GIVING AND RECEIVING

Materials:

> *Weekly Check-in*
> *"Dealing With Compliments"*

Goals:

> To teach the men the value of giving and receiving compliments; to help them iden-tify ways in which they deflect the value of compliments and ways in which they could offer compliments more effectively.

Tasks:

> 1. *Review Weekly Check-in.*
> 2. *Review homework.*
> 3. *Explain types of compliments.*
> 4. *Review handout on "Dealing with Compliments."*
> 5. *Model deflections of compliments.*
> 6. *Encourage discussion of self-talk attitudes about compliments.*
> 7. *Lead exercise in offering compliments.*
> 8. *Assign homework.*

Program:

1. Explain how assertiveness includes the ability to offer clear and direct compliments to other people—and to find ways to truly accept the compliments of others. Define compliments: generate specific examples of different kinds of compliments, including those on appearance, behavior, and basic personality.

2. Review "Dealing with Compliments." Explain the "assertive" way of dealing with compliments: accept and reward. As an exercise, ask the men to offer you a com-pliment—and then model an example of one defensive response. To make it more entertaining, ask for a different compliment from each group member until you have modeled all five defensive responses. Ask the group members to discuss per-sonal examples of these responses.

3. Now review the self-talk that makes it difficult for people to give compliments, such as, "I never got very much praise, why should I give it?" or to receive them, such as, "People will think I'm full of myself."

4. Make sure to discuss the ways in which compliments can be used in manipulative fashion, and why some people are so mistrusting of compliments. Role play examples of group members using compliments genuinely and manipulatively in their marriages.

5. Go around the room and ask each group member to offer a genuine compliment to the three group members on his right. Direct the group's attention to the ways in which compliments are both offered and received.

Homework

1. Record three compliments you receive over the next week. Describe your self-talk and your response to each of them.

   * Compliment:
     Self-Talk:
     Response:

   * Compliment:
     Self-Talk:
     Response:

   * Compliment:
     Self-Talk:
     Response:

DEALING WITH COMPLIMENTS

ASSERTIVE RESPONSE

Accepting compliments is one sign of assertiveness, which can help us feel better about ourselves. The purpose of this exercise is to examine what happens to us when we are given a sincere compliment and when we give one to another person.

Accept and Reward: This is the most assertive and positive response to compliments. It usually means saying *"Thanks. I appreciate that"* and looking pleased. The key to this style is that you feel good and you make the *other* person feel good for complimenting you. He or she will want to do it again.

DEFENSIVE RESPONSES

Refuse: *"Oh, that old thing?"* or *"I'm really messing up—I just cover it up well."* This kind of refusal gives the message that the person offering the compliment is wrong or that his perceptions are off. Is the other person likely to compliment you again?

Deflect: This involves body language: tossing the compliment away by looking down with the eyes or shrugging the shoulders. Another way is to just ignore the compliment completely and show no signs of taking it in.

Automatic Return: This is a common way that people deal with the discomfort of receiving the compliment. Here, you blurt out *"Oh, thanks, you look nice, too!"* so fast that it seems phony and forced. There is nothing wrong with offering someone else a compliment in return, but saying it too quickly or searching too hard doesn't work.

Becoming Suspicious: You know that sometimes people will try to manipulate you with compliments. If this has been done to you in the past, you may become automatically suspicious even when there is no reason to be. You may always wonder "What does she want from me now?"

Big Shot: Because the compliment makes you nervous, you cover up those feelings and say, *"Damn straight! I am the strongest dude in town! And you know—women are crazy about me! So you've got good taste!"* Who would ever want to give this guy a compliment again?

Session 24
CONFLICT WITH RESPECT AND PROBLEM-SOLVING

Materials:

> *Weekly Check-in*
> *"Conflict with Respect"*
> *"Problem-Solving"*
> *"Who Decides?"*
> *"Expectations of Marriage"*

Goals:

To introduce a cognitive structure for couple communication and problem-solving; to create a nonthreatening atmosphere in which men can reveal their specific relationship and communication difficulties.

Tasks:

> 1. *Review Weekly Check-in.*
> 2. *Review homework.*
> 3. *Review "Conflict with Respect."*
> 4. *Model and role play examples of "dealing straight," including the "wrong" way to do it.*
> 5. *Review "Problem-Solving," and role play an example.*
> 6. *Explain "Who Decides?"*
> 7. *Assign homework.*

Program:

1. Review "Conflict with Respect" Model and role play examples of each, including the "wrong" way of doing it. Use this session to review many of the communication principles the group has already learned.

2. Review the "Problem-Solving" handout. Review all the steps first, then model a problem-solving session. Model examples, role play, and reinforce techniques learned in previous sessions.

3. Briefly introduce the "Expectations of Marriage" handout for homework. Focus the discussion on the frustration that often comes from the gap between expectations and reality. **Emphasize how easy it is to project blame for this frustration onto our partners.**

Homework

1. Practice problem-solving using the "Problem-Solving" handout. Describe the problem you discussed and the solution you developed.
   Problem:
   Solution:

2. Complete the "Who Decides?" handout. Prepare to discuss this in the group.

3. Review the "Expectations of Marriage" handout and write brief answers for each question.

CONFLICT WITH RESPECT

 **Handout**

Arguments can be a useful way to solve problems, or they can be never-ending battles that can increase tension and the risk of abuse. The central theme here, as always, is respect. Can you offer your partner respect even when you're upset? The following guidelines can make a difference:

USE FAIR BEHAVIOR (RESPECT)

- Let your partner know what you want to discuss.
- All subjects are OK. Make "I statements," owning your thoughts and feelings.
- Speak one at a time and allow equal time.
- Use "active listening": reflect back what your partner is probably thinking and feeling.
- Look for compromises.
- Talk about the here-and-now.
- Refer only to the immediate problem—don't bring in the past.
- Make room for time-outs and breaks.
- Give your reasons and offer solutions.
- Admit when you're wrong.
- When you have come to an agreement, repeat it or write it down to make sure both of you are clear about it.
- Finish the argument, even if it means taking a time-out along the way.

HOW TO AVOID UNFAIR BEHAVIOR (DISRESPECT)

- Do not use name-calling or put-downs.
- Do not drag up old wounds from the past.
- Stay on track; do not go off in different directions.
- Do not threaten or intimidate.
- Do not assume that you will either win or lose this argument.
- Do not save up all your gripes to dump on your partner all at once.
- Be careful of "mind-reading" self-talk. Don't assume the most negative things about your partner. ASK!
- Do not deny the facts. Come clean.
- Do not gloat over a "victory" in getting your way.
- Do not sulk, ignore, pout, withdraw, or give your partner the silent treatment.

KEEP TRYING—THIS MAY TAKE A WHILE!

PROBLEM-SOLVING*

Handout

I. **What is the problem?**
   A. Use "I-messages" to express your needs. Do not cast blame.
   B. Listen to others' view of the problem.
   C. Make sure everyone agrees about what the problem is.
   D. Make sure others know you want a solution that will meet everyone's needs.

II. **Brainstorm for possible solutions.**
   A. Get possible solutions from others involved.
   B. Don't evaluate or discount any solutions at this point.
   C. Write down all suggested solutions.

III. **Look at the pros and cons of each possible solution.**
   A. Everyone must be honest.
   B. Do a lot of critical thinking about possible solutions.

IV. **Decide on a solution acceptable to all.**
   A. Do not push a solution on others.
   B. State the solution so everyone definitely understands it.
   C. Write down the solution so you can check later to make sure that's what each agreed upon.

V. **Put the solution into action.**
   A. Talk about who will do what and when.
   B. Trust everyone to carry out his or her part.
   C. Promote individual responsibility by avoiding reminders, nagging, or monitoring.
   D. If someone is not responsible, he or she may need to be confronted using "I messages."

VI. **Evaluate the solution.**
   A. Modify the solution if necessary.
   B. Check out each person's feelings about the solution.
   C. If after a fair amount of time the solution is not working, try another mutually agreed upon solution.

---

*Adapted with permission from Geffner & Mantooth, 1995. May not be reproduced without permission.

WHO DECIDES?*

 **Handout**

Check below whether you think an item should be your decision, your wife's or partner's decision, or open to negotiation. Remember that there are no right or wrong answers here—as long as both partners agree about the decision-making process.

	Your decision	Mostly yours	Joint decision	Mostly hers	Your partner's decision
1. Which friends can she spend time with?					
2. Which friends can you spend time with?					
3. Can she drink on certain occasions?					
4. Can you drink on certain occasions?					
5. Who decides on a sitter for the children?					
6. Will she get a job?					
7. Will you get a job?					
8. Will she go to school?					
9. Will you go to school?					
10. Which friends or relatives can visit your home?					
11. How will the children be disciplined?					
12. What is your paycheck spent on?					
13. What is her paycheck spent on?					

---

* Adapted with permission from Pence & Paymar, 1993.

EXPECTATIONS OF MARRIAGE

 **Handout**

1. When you got married or started your relationship, what were your dreams and hopes? Which have been met? Which have failed?

2. Do you remember a time in your marriage when you felt very happy and fulfilled? Have you ever felt angry at your wife or partner because she seemed to change? Does it seem like she broke a promise by not continuing to make you feel good?

3. What kind of marriage did your parents have? How did that affect your own expectations? Did you want it to be the same? Or did you want it to be very different?

4. Are you angry with your wife or partner for not being like "mom" or "dad"? Are you angry at your spouse for being <u>too much</u> like "mom" or "dad"?

5. When something goes wrong in your family, are you worried about the disapproval from your parents or other family members? Do you think you are disappointing someone?

6. Perhaps most importantly: did you witness or were you the victim of physical abuse yourself? How does this affect your own expectations of family life?

Session 25

EXPECTATIONS OF MARRIAGE: OLD AND NEW

Materials:

Weekly Check-in
"Expectations of Marriage" (from Session 24)
"Power and Control"
"Equality"

Goals:

To understand male power and the benefits of equality; to review the original expectations of marriage for each group member; to become aware of the gap between the idealized expectations and the real relationship.

Tasks:

1. *Review Weekly Check-in.*
2. *Review the "Power and Control" wheel.*
3. *Review the "Equality" wheel.*
4. *Review homework on "Expectations of Marriage."*
5. *Assign homework.*

Program:

1. We all like to feel respected. Self-respect and the respect of others are at the end of the road called "equality." Along with a vision of power, the men need a vision of equality on which to fix their sights.

   Review the "Power and Control" wheel. Compare these concepts to the "House of Abuse" (page 47). Next, draw or show the "Equality" wheel. Ask each man to describe two or three areas where he thinks he needs to work to improve the equality in his relationship with women. Encourage the men to describe specific actions they would take toward their goals.

2. Discuss the beliefs each man has about how marriage "should" be. Review the homework handout on "Expectations of Marriage." Focus the discussion on the frustration that often results from the gap between expectations and reality.

Emphasize how easy it is to project blame for this frustration onto our partners. This is one of the most important messages we can offer to help these men take more "psychological" responsibility for their own pain. Here, it is best to operate from the "pacing and leading" model: first, show respect for the feelings that these men (like all of us) have about disappointments in relationships, and second, coach them about how to deal with these feelings without turning against their partners or wives. Stress that men and women are all in this together.

Homework

1. Complete the "Sexual Meaning Questionnaire."
2. Read the article "I Raped My Wife."

POWER AND CONTROL WHEEL

 Handout

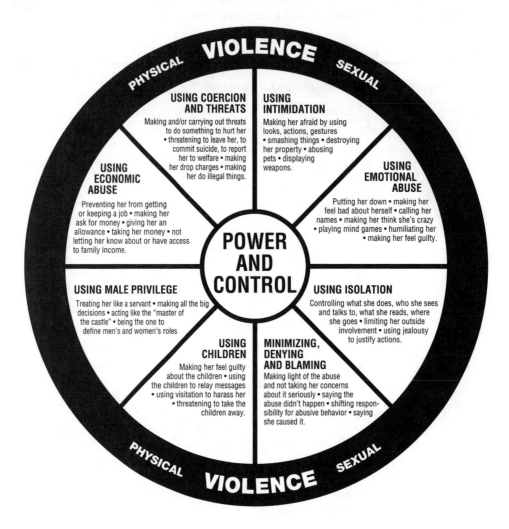

EQUALITY WHEEL

 Handout

NON-THREATENING BEHAVIOR

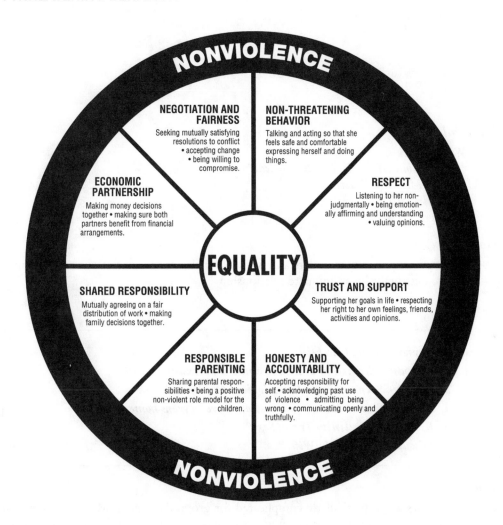

Session 26
SEX

Materials:

> *Weekly Check-in*
> *"Sexual Abuse: Psychological & Physical"*
> *"Sexual Meaning Questionnaire"*
> *"Masculinity Traps: Sex"*
> *"I Raped My Wife"*

Goal:

> To help group members understand ways in which sexual expectations and demands can be destructive in an intimate relationship

Tasks:

> 1. *Review Weekly Check-in.*
> 2. *Introduce definition of sexual abuse and sexual assault.*
> 3. *Review "Sexual Abuse: Psychological & Physical."*
> 4. *Review "Sexual Meaning Questionnaire" (from homework).*
> 5. *Review "Masculinity Traps: Sex."*
> 6. *Discuss "I Raped My Wife."*

Program:

1. This session is particularly complicated for group discussion. Many of the group members, who may have become less defensive about general actions of psychological and physical abuse, may continue to maintain considerable defensiveness about examples of what we are describing as sexual abuse.

   Some of this is simply from ignorance or lack of awareness about why certain behaviors qualify as abusive. First of all, it is important to simply define sexual abuse: **any unwanted touching or other sexual behavior is a form of abuse.** If it involves intercourse, it is rape. If it involves physical force, it is sexual assault. It doesn't matter if the assaulter is drunk, stoned, or feeling pressured by his friends—it is still rape or sexual assault. And it doesn't matter if the two parties know each other, have had sex before, or even if they are married. It is still considered rape or sexual assault.

2. With these definitions in mind, review the "Sexual Abuse: Psychological & Physical" handout. Discuss the variety of ways in which sexual behaviors can represent an abuse of power in the relationship. Obviously, not all of the examples on the list are criminal offenses—but they represent a continuum of sexually abusive behaviors.

3. As you guide this discussion, be especially sensitive to the embarrassment or discomfort that the group members are likely to experience. Some may joke around or join in laughter with degrading comments toward women. Although it is important to set a different tone in this group, be careful about confronting too intensely—unless all else fails. Power struggles will doom this group discussion. Set an example by maintaining a serious tone yourself. Calmly remind the men of the importance in talking these issues in ways that do not degrade or generalize. If they are able to describe examples of some of these destructive sexual behaviors in "others," this may be an acceptable way to generate valuable discussion and reflection.

4. Review the "Sexual Meaning Questionnaire" and "I Raped My Wife" (from last session's homework) and "Masculinity Traps: Sex." It is especially important to focus on issues of entitlement and perceived peer pressure in this discussion. Refer back to previous discussion on jealousy and misinterpretations; remind the men, through examples, how crucial their self-talk is when they encounter some form of sexual frustration.

SEXUAL ABUSE: PSYCHOLOGICAL & PHYSICAL

 **Handout**

Sexual abuse is one of the rooms from the House of Abuse that is especially difficult to talk about. Sometimes it is even difficult to know that it is taking place. Below is a sample of different forms of abusive sexual behaviors, both psychological and physical. If you can, try to be honest with yourself about which of these you may have used at some point in your relationships.

PUT-DOWNS

- Making jokes about women in your partner's presence
- Checking out other women in her presence
- Making sexual put-down jokes
- Comparing her body to other women or to pictures in magazines
- Criticizing sexual performance
- Blaming her if you don't feel satisfied with sex
- Using sexual labels: calling her a "slut" or calling her "frigid"

MIND-GAMES

- Telling her that agreeing to sex is the only way she can prove she has been faithful or that she still loves you
- Revealing intimate details about her to others
- Withholding sex and affection only to gain control over the other person
- Engaging in sexual affairs

PRESSURE

- Always wanting sex
- Expecting sex whenever you want it
- Demanding sex with threats
- Talking her into stripping or talking sexually in a way that feels humiliating to her
- Talking her into watching sex or pornography when this is offensive to her
- Talking her into touching others when this is offensive to her

FORCE

- Forcing touch
- Forcing sex while she's sleeping
- Touching her in ways that are uncomfortable to her
- Forcing uncomfortable sex
- Forcing sex after physical abuse
- Sex for the purpose of hurting (use of objects/weapons)

MASCULINITY TRAPS: SEX

 **Handout**

MASCULINITY TRAPS

- "I deserve to have sex upon demand."

- "If my wife or partner doesn't put out, it means she's trying to hurt me."

- "Real men get laid all the time."

- "I've had a hard day. I deserve some rewards!"

THE BIG PICTURE

"Sex involves the needs of two people, not just one."

"There are many reasons why my wife or partner may not be in the mood for sex."

"Many men talk big—real men respect the needs and individuality of someone they love."

"I can't expect my wife to always be available exactly when I need her."

SEXUAL MEANING QUESTIONNAIRE

 **Handout**

Rate the importance of the various functions of sex in your life by circling the number that best describes how you feel about each item.

Function of sex in your life	Not Important						Very Important
1. Produce children	1	2	3	4	5	6	7
2. Orgasm for me	1	2	3	4	5	6	7
3. Orgasm for my partner	1	2	3	4	5	6	7
4. Reassurance of my masculinity	1	2	3	4	5	6	7
5. Reassure my partner of her femininity	1	2	3	4	5	6	7
6. Reassurance of my heterosexuality	1	2	3	4	5	6	7
7. Reassurance of her heterosexuality	1	2	3	4	5	6	7
8. Reassurance that I'm OK sexually	1	2	3	4	5	6	7
9. Reassure my partner that she is OK sexually	1	2	3	4	5	6	7
10. Expression of love by me	1	2	3	4	5	6	7
11. Expression of love for me	1	2	3	4	5	6	7
12. Way to release tension	1	2	3	4	5	6	7
13. Way to show off my body	1	2	3	4	5	6	7
14. Way to prove my sexual skills	1	2	3	4	5	6	7
15. Recreation	1	2	3	4	5	6	7
16. Part of relationship responsibility	1	2	3	4	5	6	7
17. Companionship	1	2	3	4	5	6	7
18. Warmth	1	2	3	4	5	6	7
19. Way of trapping a partner	1	2	3	4	5	6	7
20. Way to have fun	1	2	3	4	5	6	7
21. Way to make up after argument or conflict	1	2	3	4	5	6	7
22. Way of exercising power and control	1	2	3	4	5	6	7
23. Way of curing boredom	1	2	3	4	5	6	7
24. Because I haven't had sex for a while	1	2	3	4	5	6	7
25. Way to reduce stress	1	2	3	4	5	6	7

I RAPED MY WIFE*

Handout

GLENN'S STORY (AS TOLD TO HIS THERAPIST)

Glenn talked about several major areas of his life during a marathon session that lasted over three hours. He expressed regret that he and his father had never been close. He felt disgusted with his compulsion to please people and the fact that he had no true friends. He was disappointed in his selfishness; he heard himself saying "my" much too often. He experienced gross ambivalence over the way he still seemed attached to his mother's apron-strings.

When we reached the topic of sex, Glenn was guilt ridden and embarrassed. He started to talk about himself as if he were the world's greatest lover. But with a gentle nudge he reversed his "macho man" routine, confided that it was difficult for him to accept his sexuality openly and honestly. He recounted a recent event that he thought proved he was "coming out of the closet" and accepting the spontaneity of his sexuality.

"I came home early one day last week. Dana was dusting the furniture and looking very sexy in her cut-off jeans. I walked up behind her and grabbed her"—Glenn opened his hands and flexed his fingers, recreating the manner in which he had begun his "foreplay."

"I pushed her over the dining room table and started unzipping her jeans. She pushed my hands away saying she didn't want to do it there. The kids were gone for a while, so I knew we had time. I kept undressing her. She told me to stop, but I knew I would make her like it."

As Glenn continued, his pride was as great as his boastfulness. Our emotions went in opposite directions. He got excited, I was saddened.

"It didn't last very long. I don't think I made it for even thirty seconds, but it was good."

I sat in silence, replaying the essence of what Glenn had just told me. It was evident that he was totally unaware of the nature of his actions. In the softest, most supportive tone I could manage, I hit him with harsh reality. "You raped your wife, Glenn. Maybe not legally, but physically and emotionally, you raped Dana."

His face turned ashen, his mouth dropped open, and his eyes wide with awe, stared off into oblivion. He didn't move; I don't think he could have. Then small droplets of tears formed a glaze over his eyes, and he whispered, "Oh my God!"

Thousands of floodlights had been switched on inside his head. Suddenly, hundreds of things he had never realized he knew were visible to his mind's eye. Glenn was in shock. Every four or five seconds he whispered, "Oh my God!" Every fifteen or twenty seconds he looked at me, each time more tears forming in his eyes. His incredulity lasted over five minutes, a lifetime in psychotherapy.

Glenn choked over his words. "Of course—that's exactly what I did. I raped my wife. The only person I truly care about. Damn, I'm a helluva guy, aren't I?" His self-criticism was filled with overwhelming guilt.

More silence.

The shock of his insight pulled Glenn all the way down. "I've hit bottom. Everything Dana has been saying is true. I've been too damn stupid to see it. She tells me I don't really know how to love her, that I don't respect her. She

---

*Used with permission from Kiley, 1983.

says I don't know how to express my feelings. She tells me I need to grow up. I listened to all those things, but I never <u>heard</u> them."

He paused, his mind racing. "How do I recover from this? How do I make up for what I did? Where do I start?" He was searching desperately for relief from his guilt.

"There are several things you need to do. First, knock off the guilt. It's useless. Second, dedicate yourself to the process of growing up. Psychotherapy can help you immensely in that area. Third, go home, hug your wife, tell her you love her, and let her know that things are going to change."

Session 27
KIDS

Materials:

> *Weekly Check-in*
> *The Great Santini: Scene IV*
> *"When Kids See Their Parents Fight . . ."*
> *"Questions for Kids"*
> *"Kid Stories"*

Goal:

> To help the group members develop increased understanding of the effects of domestic violence on children and empathy for their children.

Tasks:

> 1. *Review Weekly Check-in.*
> 2. *Discuss the effects of domestic violence on children.*
> 3. *Play The Great Santini: Scene IV and discuss.*
> 4. *Review "When Kids See Their Parents Fight . . ."*
> 5. *Review and role play "Questions for Kids."*
> 6. *Explain "Kid Stories" and assign homework.*

Program:

1. Discuss the effects on kids of witnessing domestic violence. Begin by explaining that abusive fighting—verbal and physical—affects not only the adults, but also the children, who witness it. Emphasize that children usually have excellent radar for tuning in to this behavior, even if the parents are "sure" it is all happening behind closed doors.

2. Play *The Great Santini: Scene IV* (begin at 1:28:29 and end at 1:29:57) and discuss. Review the ways in which each child has his or her own specific reaction to the violence. Identify self-talk for the children and the parents.

3. Review "When Kids See Their Parents Fight . . ." Ask the group members to identify any of these symptoms they have noticed in their own kids. Also ask them

to recall experiences when they were growing up and witnessed violence between their parents.

4. Review "Questions for Kids." Select a group member to play the role of his child who has witnessed violence. As this child, he answers these questions, asked in detail by the group leaders and group members. Review the self-talk and emotions. Repeat with all group members who have kids.

Homework

1. Complete the "Kid Stories" handout and bring it for group review next session.

WHEN KIDS SEE THEIR PARENTS FIGHT . . .

 Handout

When kids see their parents fight they will often display symptoms like these, without always being able to tell you what is bothering them:

- SLEEP PROBLEMS: fears of going to sleep, nightmares, dreams of danger
- MYSTERIOUS ACHES AND PAINS: headaches, stomachaches, medical problems like asthma, arthritis, ulcers
- FEARS: anxiety about being hurt or killed, fears of going to school or of separating from mother, worrying, difficulties concentrating and paying attention
- BEHAVIOR PROBLEMS: abusing drugs or alcohol, suicide attempts or engaging in dangerous behavior, eating problems, bed-wetting or regression to earlier developmental stages, acting perfect, overachieving, behaving like small adults
- PEOPLE PROBLEMS: losing interest in people, fighting or abusing others, outbursts of temper, tantrums
- EMOTIONAL PROBLEMS: losing interest in activities, feeling lonely

QUESTIONS FOR KIDS*

 **Handout**

In this exercise, group members take turns role-playing being the child in their house who has witnessed violence. Other group members interview these "kids" about their experiences.

1. What kinds of things do your mom and dad fight about?

2. What happens when your mom or dad gets angry or your parents fight? Can you describe any fights between your parents that you saw yourself? What did you see or hear during the fight? What was it like for you afterwards (e.g., did you see your mother's injuries or the house torn apart)? What were your reactions?

3. What do you do if your parents push, shove, or hit each other? Do you leave the room or go outside?

4. Can you describe any fights between your parents in which you were caught in the middle, or when you tried to stop them? What happened?

5. Do they ever fight about you? How does this make you feel (scared, confused, sad, mad)?

6. Do you talk to anybody about this?

7. How do you handle your feelings since this has happened? Do you ever feel like hurting yourself or anyone else?

8. In an emergency for you or your parents, who would you call? Where could you go?

---

*Adapted with permission from the Family Violence Prevention Fund's publication entitled *Domestic Violence: A National Curriculum for Family Preservation Practitioners,* written by Susan Schecter, M.S.W., and Anne L. Ganley, Ph.D. May not be reproduced without permission.

KID STORIES*

Handout

1. **You are a 14-year-old boy,** and you really like playing basketball more than anything else. Your dad has been getting drunk lately. He comes home and hits your mom, and he breaks things after he thinks the kids have gone to sleep. Your sister has started using drugs and running away. One day after school, your mom tells you that you and your brothers and sister are moving to another town, across the state, and that you will be living with your aunt and uncle. Your mom tells you that she can't trust your dad anymore and that you kids might be the next to get hurt. You've never seen your dad hit your brothers and sister, and he's never hit you.

   ■ How would you feel when you heard about your mom's plans?

   ■ How would you feel toward your mother?

   ■ How would you feel toward your father?

2. **You are a 10-year-old girl** who's been really screwing up at school lately. Your dad is constantly on your case; nothing you do is right. You know your mom has been spending a lot of money, and he is always yelling at her about it. One time he locked her out of the house, and she had to stay outside in the rain until you snuck around the back to let her in. She yells right back at him, calling him bad names. Sometimes she even throws things at him and you can hear things breaking. You and your mom have left a couple of times for a few days, but she always comes back. It's hard for you to sleep. You want this to stop, and you ask if you can live with somebody else for a while.

   ■ How would you feel toward your mother?

   ■ How would you feel toward your father?

---

*Adapted with permission from the Family Violence Prevention Fund's publication entitled *Domestic Violence: A National Curriculum for Family Preservation Practitioners,* written by Susan Schecter, M.S.W., and Anne L. Ganley, Ph.D. May not be reproduced without permission.

Session 28
PARENTS

Materials:

> *Weekly Check-in*
> *"Listening to Kids"*
> *"Tips for Parents & Kids"*
> *"Selecting the Right Approach"*

Goals:

> To help group members identify their own attitudes toward and approaches with their children and to develop new skills in communication and problem-solving.

Tasks:

> *1. Review Weekly Check-in.*
> *2. Review "Listening to Kids."*
> *3. Review "Tips for Parents & Kids."*
> *4. Review "Selecting the Right Approach" and assign homework.*

Program:

1. Introduce the topic of parenting. Ask each of the men the name, age, and sex of each of their children and write them on the board.

2. Review "Listening to Kids." Use this handout to stimulate discussion about the self-talk, needs, and feelings that kids have. Remind them of their skills in active listening. Role play different "shut down" and "open up" responses and examine the internal reactions of the kids in this dialogue.

3. Review "Tips for Parents & Kids." Discuss each of these guidelines. When discussing the kids' guidelines, have the group role play their own kids having this discussion.

4. Review "Selecting the Right Approach." This section is most likely to stir up controversy as the men declare their views on discipline, punishment, spanking, talking back, etc. It is important to remain respectful of their points of view while still

presenting new models for handling problems. Don't make the mistake of implying that this "right" approach to consequences—or any other skills in parenting that we propose—can serve as "magic." Any group members with kids will know that there is no such thing.

As part of a review of self-talk patterns, help the group members examine their own reasons for reacting to their kids in certain ways. Discuss the differences in motivation between wanting to punish for doing something wrong and offering consequences with the goal of correction. Which of the following might apply?

- *"I want to make it clear who's in charge."*
- *"I want to open up communication between me and my daughter or son."*
- *"It's time to express <u>my</u> feelings."*
- *"Nobody should be allowed to treat me like this."*
- *"I want to model positive behaviors for my kids."*
- *"I want us to solve this problem together."*
- *"I'm afraid of losing this kid."*

Homework

1. Answer the questions from "Selecting The Right Approach" handout.

LISTENING TO KIDS*

 **Handout**

If you want to open up communication with kids, you need to read between the lines of what they say. Your response needs to open things up, not shut it down. As you review this list, remember the principles of active listening.

Child Says:	Shut Down:	Open Up:
I'm never going to play with her again!	Why don't you forget it? She probably didn't mean it.	You're really angry with her.
I can't do it!	Now don't talk like that! You just got started!	It seems very difficult to you.
I wish I could go along. He always gets to go everywhere.	We've discussed this before. Stop fussing.	It seems unfair to you.
Look at my new model!	That's nice. Now will you please go!	You're pleased with your work on it.
I don't want to go to school. Billy is mean!	Everyone has to go to school. It's the law.	You're afraid Billy will pick on you today.
You're the meanest mother in the whole world!	Don't you ever talk to me that way!	You're very angry with me.

For each remark, give an example of a "shut down" and an "open up."

1. I don't like vegetables, and I'm not going to eat them.

2. Our teacher is crabby.

3. I don't want to go to bed! It's too early.

4. I'm not going to wear my raincoat. Nobody in my class wears a stupid old raincoat.

TIPS FOR PARENTS & KIDS

Handout

In a recent communication survey of pre-teens (5th through 8th graders) conducted by the Philips Consumer Communications Company, researchers discovered the following information:

- Most parents (58%) and almost three-quarters of their kids (73%) say they spend less than an hour a day in conversation; nearly half the kids (46%) and about a quarter of the parents (27%) say they spend less than a half-hour a day talking to each other.
- Most parents underestimate the maturity of their kids and have misconceptions about what's important to them. Parents say the top priorities for their kids are: (1) fun, (2) friends, and (3) looks. Kids say their top priorities are: (1) their future, (2) their schoolwork, and (3) family matters.
- Only 1 in 5 kids (20%) say it is very easy to talk to their parents about things that really matter; more than a quarter (26%) say it is "somewhat difficult" or "very difficult" to talk about such things; about half of the kids (53%) say it is "somewhat easy."
- Most kids (57%) say that their parents don't always give them a chance to explain themselves. Most parents (51%) feel the same way—that their kids don't always give them a chance to explain themselves.
- Kids are more interested in the opposite sex than their parents think—almost two-thirds (62%) of kids say the opposite sex is an important issue, while only about half (52%) of parents think their kids are interested in boyfriends or girlfriends.

TIPS FOR KIDS

LISTEN TO BE HEARD: Acknowledge your parents' point of view on an issue and they'll be more likely to listen to your point of view. In the end, it will help you better understand each other and think of creative solutions and compromises.

PLAN AHEAD: Think about what your parents will object to and how you will answer them. Try to come up with alternative solutions to a problem you're having instead of just one solution and present them to your parents. They'll be impressed.

BE POLITE: It's simple but it's true. If you yell and scream, it will remind your parents of when you were a little kid, and they'll probably treat you that way. If you're polite, they'll probably pay more attention to your opinions. Politeness rules.

JUST SAY IT: All communication involves taking risks. Even though it may be hard, sometimes the best thing you can do when you have a problem is to gather your courage up and talk about it.

WATCH YOUR BODY LANGUAGE: Sometimes your facial expressions and posture say more to the people you're talking to than the words you use. Think about what you say—and how you say it.

TIPS FOR PARENTS

MAKE THE TIME: In today's complex world, it's more important than ever to set aside time to talk. That doesn't mean you have to hold a formal meeting. Sometimes the best discussions take place while you're driving the car or puttering around the kitchen.

LISTEN TO THE LITTLE STUFF: Kids will talk to you if they know you're going to listen whether they discuss heavy issues such as sex and drugs or everyday things like what happened in school. If your kids know you're listening, they're more likely to trust you enough to talk about everything in their life.

LISTEN BETWEEN THE LINES: Because a lot of kids find it hard to talk to their parents about things that really matter, parents have to pay special attention to what their kids are trying to say. It helps to pay particular attention to emotions—not just the emotion itself, but its intensity, too.

ASK THEIR OPINION: Few things please children (or anybody else) more than being asked their opinion. You don't have to ask about important issues all the time, either.

DON'T INTERRUPT: Kids say that when they talk, their parents often or sometimes don't give them a chance to explain themselves. It's a good idea to give your children some extra time to explain their opinion or desires, even if you think you know what they're going to say.

SELECTING THE RIGHT APPROACH*

 **Handout**

In order to decide how to handle a problem with a child, you must first figure out whose problem it is. Then you can select from different strategies, such as natural and logical consequences, ignoring the behavior, expressing your feelings, exploring alternatives, etc. Study the examples in this chart; then fill out your own answers to the questions.

Problem	Who Owns Problem?	Right Approach
Child borrows father's tools and does not return them	Parent	*I-Message*—"When you don't return my tools, I get upset because I need them"; or *Logical Consequence*—Deny child loan of tools next time she wants to borrow them.
Child is upset about failing test.	Child	*Reflective Listening*—"You're very sad about failing the test." *Explore Alternatives*—"What are some things you can do next time you have a test?"
Child neglects homework.	Child	*Logical Consequence*—Allow child to face consequences from teacher.
Toddler touches light socket.	Parent	*Logical Consequence*—Place child in playpen for short time. Then let child out. If child approaches socket again, place in playpen for longer period.

Who owns the problem? What is the right approach?

1. Child does not lock up his or her bicycle.

2. Child does not return milk carton to refrigerator.

3. Infant in high chair throws food.

RELAPSE PREVENTION

Sessions 29 and 30

MOST VIOLENT AND/OR MOST FRIGHTENING INCIDENT

Materials:

> *Weekly Check-in*

Goal:

> To review the most disturbing incident in the relationship <u>that the group member has committed</u>, so that he can recognize the impact on himself and on others.

Tasks:

> 1. *Review Weekly Check-in.*
> 2. *Review most violent and/or most frightening incident with group member.*
> 3. *Review affect and self-talk during incident.*
> 4. *Continue process with as many group members as possible.*

Program:

1. Ask a group member to review, in detail, the most disturbing abusive incident in his relationship <u>that he has committed</u>. This is not necessarily the most physically injurious event, but rather the one that stands out as the most emotionally upsetting. Pick somebody who you think will be able to do this well, providing a positive model for the others. It is very important for the group member to describe this incident as vividly as possible, in the first person present, as if it were happening in slow motion.

2. The group member should be asked to describe, at various intervals, the following information:

   - his self-talk
   - his emotions
   - his physical state

   Particularly important is his affect. You may need to say repeatedly, *"Describe how you are feeling at this point."* The goal here is to diminish as much of the original denial and minimization as possible. This is an opportunity to go into more depth with these issues—particularly with some of the new skills and information that they now have.

3. Insist that the group member also identify the following, using the skills learned in the Empathy Training (Session 21) and Kids (Session 27) exercises:

   ■ partner's and child's self-talk
   ■ partner's and child's emotion
   ■ partner's and child's physical state

4. Continue with all group members during this session and the following one.

Session 31
PREVENTION PLAN I

Materials:

Weekly Check-in
"Prevention Plan"

Goal:

To integrate the variety of coping skills in a rehearsal for challenging situations.

Tasks:

1. *Review Weekly Check-in.*
2. *Explain theory of "Prevention Plan."*
3. *Review basic steps of "Prevention Plan."*
4. *Guide one group member through development of "Prevention Plan."*
5. *Role play one situation while group members rehearse new response.*
6. *Assign homework.*

Program:

1. Explain that the "Prevention Plan" is based on a treatment called "cue therapy," which was originally developed to treat cocaine abusers in a Veterans' Center. Clinical research showed that, even though the patients were exposed to many excellent treatments, many relapsed because they could not resist the old familiar "cues" that triggered the familiar drug pattern. Cue therapy was introduced so that they could carefully rehearse exposure to these cues while practicing many alternative coping strategies.

2. Ask for a volunteer to identify a cue or trigger for his own aggression. Then guide him through each of the different coping strategies. At the completion, he should have generated one strategy from each category.

3. Now role play the cue situation and ask the volunteer to practice each of the coping strategies. Explain that, in real situations, it is rarely practical to use all of these. However, it is valuable to be equipped with as many as possible just in case. This is an advanced version of the "Responsibility Plan" (see Session 2).

4. Ask each group member to decide on his own most difficult cue to resist and to generate coping strategies. Rehearse as many of these as possible.

Homework

1. Complete the "Prevention Plan" handout and bring it for group review next session.

PREVENTION PLAN*

 Handout

Purpose: To prepare you for future situations when you might be tempted to become abusive with your partner.

Behavior I'm Trying to Manage: _____

Cues: 1. _____
   2. _____
   3. _____

COPING STRATEGIES:

1. Scare yourself image—Example: Remember the damage to your family, remember being arrested, etc.

and/or

2. Support yourself image—Example: Focus on a positive image, such as how proud you will feel if you are able to control your reactions.

and/or

3. Relaxation techniques—Example: Deep breathing, progressive muscle relaxation, etc.

and/or

4. Fun and Distraction—Example: Listening to music, playing basketball, etc.

and/or

5. Self-talk—Example: "This isn't worth it," "Nobody's perfect," "I want to keep my life together."

and/or

6. Friends—Example: Call a friend, crisis line, therapist, sponsor, or family member.

and/or

7. Problem-solving—Example: Talk calmly and respectfully to your wife or partner about what upset you.

and/or

8. Use a time-out if necessary.

_____

Session 32
PREVENTION PLAN II

Materials:

> *Weekly Check-in*
> *"Transfer of Change"*

Goal:

> To review the skills learned throughout the program and to make specific plans for dealing with stressful situations more effectively.

Tasks:

> 1. *Review Weekly Check-in.*
> 2. *Review homework.*
> 3. *Practice "time machine" technique with one or more group members.*
> 4. *Discuss what the men have learned in the program.*
> 5. *Discuss "Transfer of Change" and follow steps in the group.*
> 6. *Role play "negative" influences: Who should you <u>not</u> talk to?*

Program:

1. All of the exercises in this session facilitate the men's transition from the structure of this group to the use of these skills and insights on their own.

2. Review the Prevention Plans that each group member prepared as homework and discuss how effective they were at trying them over the past week.

3. Use the "time machine" technique to help the group members project themselves into the future. This is a way of developing clearer goals and anticipating possible pitfalls. Ask for a volunteer. Have this man choose a date in the future, such as a year from today. Using any dramatic means with which you feel comfortable, help the group imagine that he is being projected via time machine to that date. When he "wakes up," the group interviews him about his life on his future date. Specific questions about how he has managed to communicate better or work things out with his wife or partner are very helpful. Help him keep the material realistic.

When he is finished, bring him back to the present. Repeat this process with several more men if time allows.

4. Ask each group member to discuss what he has learned here that will have the most impact on him in the future.

5. Discuss "Transfer of Change" and follow the steps in the group. Each member should take several minutes to devise a plan. Then share the plans with entire group. The group members should help evaluate the plan of each member. Is it complete? Is it realistic? How can group members help each other to maintain change?

6. Who should you <u>not</u> talk to? (thanks to James Reavis, Psy.D., for developing this technique): Discuss how important peer groups are in maintaining new attitudes and behaviors. Ask the group to role play "negative" influences on one group member who is having problems with his relationship. Group members should challenge him by saying some of the following:

- *"You can't let her get away with that crap!"*
- *"Prove to her who's in charge!"*
- *"Just lie to her, man—you know how they all are!"*

The selected group member should practice his response to this.

TRANSFER OF CHANGE

 **Handout**

"Transfer of change" techniques help you apply what you have learned in group to problem situations outside the group. Actually, we have used many of these techniques already. Without Transfer of Change, what you learned in the group would have been only an interesting exercise with *no* application to your life.

Consider the possibilities available to you:

- Join a self-help group, such as AA.
- Teach the assertiveness principles to others.
- Maintain buddy contacts.
- Join another counseling group.
- Prepare for an unsympathetic environment (partner who doesn't communicate well/buddies who talk you into "male privilege" attitudes).
- Prepare for personal setbacks. Have back-up coping statements ready for times when techniques don't work.
- Predict specific roadblocks you may face. Have a "road map" ready to handle those situations, which includes a plan of action, techniques you could use, self-statements that would be helpful.
- Keep a diary of successes and problem areas.
- Regularly review the techniques you have learned. Decide which ones might work for you.

WHAT ARE YOUR CHANGE PLANS FOR THE NEXT MONTH?

In relation to yourself?
Example: "I will write down my self-talk whenever I am angry."

_____

_____

_____

_____

_____

_____

In relation to others?
Example: "I will set an appointment each week to discuss problems with my wife or partner."

_____

_____

_____

_____

_____

_____

WHAT ARE YOUR CHANGE PLANS FOR THE NEXT YEAR?

In relation to yourself?

Example: "I will practice relaxation daily so I will have it ready when I need it."

_____

_____

_____

_____

_____

_____

In relation to others?

Example: "I will encourage my wife or partner to develop friendships and I will try not to feel threatened."

_____

_____

_____

_____

_____

_____

REFERENCES

Amherst H. Wilder Foundation. (1995). *On the level: Foundations for violence-free living*. St. Paul, MN: Amherst H. Wilder Foundation.

Bandura, A. (1973). *Aggression: A social learning analysis*. Englewood Cliffs, NJ: Prentice-Hall.

Beck, A. T., & Freeman, A. (1990). *Cognitive therapy of personality disorders*. New York: Guilford.

Bedrosian, R. C. (1982). Using cognitive systems intervention in the treatment of marital violence. In L. R. Barnhill (Ed.), *Clinical approaches to family violence*. Rockville, MD: Aspen.

Bernstein, D. A., & Borkevec, T. D. (1973). *Progressive relaxation training*. Champaign, IL: Research Press.

Bowker, L. H. (1983). *Beating wife-beating*. Lexington, MA: Heath.

Brannen, S. J., & Rubin, A. (1996). Comparing the effectiveness of gender-specific and couples groups in a court-mandated spouse abuse treatment program. *Research on Social Work Practice, 6*(4), 405–424.

Browne, K., Saunders, D., & Staeker, K. (1997). Process-psychodynamic groups for men who batter: A brief treatment model. *Families in Society: The Journal of Contemporary Human Services,* May/June, 265–71.

Browne, A. (1987) *When battered women kill*. New York: Free Press.

Carrillo, R., & Tello, J. (Eds). (1998). *Family violence and men of color: Healing the wounded male spirit*. NY: Springer.

Deffenbacher, J. L., McNamara, K., Stark, R. S., & Sabadell, P. M. (1990). A comparison of cognitive-behavioral and process-oriented group counseling for general anger reduction. *Journal of Counseling & Development, 69*(2), 167–172.

Dinkmeyer, D., & McKay, G. (1989). *The parents' handbook: Systematic training for effective parenting*. Circle Pines, MN: American Guidance Service.

Dutton, D. (1998). *The abusive personality: Violence and control in intimate relationships*. New York: Guilford.

Dutton, D., with Golant, S. (1995). *The batterer: A psychological profile*. New York: Basic Books.

Dutton, D. G., & Holtzworth-Munroe, A. (1997). The role of early trauma in males who assault their wives. In *Rochester symposium on developmental psychology: Vol. 8. Developmental perspectives on trauma: Theory, research, and intervention* (pp. 379–401). Rochester, NY: University of Rochester Press.

Dutton, D., van Ginkel, C., & Strazomski, A. (1995). The role of shame and guilt in the intergenerational transmission of abusiveness. *Violence and Victims, 10*(2), 121–31.

D'Zurilla, T., & Goldfried, M. (1971). Problem solving and behavior modification. *Journal of Abnormal Psychology, 78,* 107–126.

Eddy, M. J., & Myers, T. (1984). *Helping men who batter: A profile of programs in the U.S.* Austin, TX: Texas Department of Human Resources.

Edleson, J. L., & Tolman, R. M. (1992). *Intervention for men who batter.* Thousand Oaks, CA: Sage.

Ellis, A. (1977). *How to live with—and without—anger.* New York: Reader's Digest Press.

Erickson, M., & Rossi, E. (1979) *Hypnotherapy: An exploratory casebook.* New York: Irvington.

Fagan, J. (1996). *The criminalization of domestic violence: Promises and limits.* Washington, DC: U.S. Dept. of Justice, Office of Justice Programs. National Institute of Justice.

Fischer, G. (1986). College student attitudes toward forcible date rape. *Journal of Sex Education and Therapy, 12,* 42–46.

Ganley, A. (1981). *Court-madated counseling for men who batter: A three-day workshop.* Washington, DC: Center for Women Policy Studies.

Geffner, R., & Mantooth, C. (1995). *A psychoeducational model for ending wife/partner abuse: A program manual for treating individuals and couples.* Tyler, TX: Family Violence and Sexual Assault Institute.

Gilligan, S. (1987). *Therapeutic trances.* New York: Brunner/Mazel.

Gondolf, E. W. (1999). MCMI-III results for batterer program participants in four cities. Less "pathological" than expected. *Journal of Family Violence; Vol 14*(1), 1–17.

Gondolf, E. W. & Russell, D. M. (1987). *Man to man: A guide for men in abusive relationships.* Bradenton, FL: Human Services Institute.

Gottman, J. (1994). *Why marriages succeed and fail.* New York: Simon & Schuster.

Gottman, J., Jacobson, N., Rushe, R., Shortt, J., Babcock, J., La Taillade, J., & Waltz, J. (1995). The relationship between heart rate activity, emotionally aggressive behavior, and general violence in batterers. *Journal of Family Psychology, 9,* 227–248.

Hamberger, L. K., & Potente, T. (1994). Counseling heterosexual women arrested for domestic violence: Implications for theory and practice. *Violence & Victims, 9*(2), 125–137.

Hare, R. (1993). *Without conscience.* New York: Pocket Books.

Harway, M., & Evans, K. (1996). Working in groups with men who batter. In M. Andronico (Ed.), *Men in groups: Insights, interventions, and psychoeducational work* (pp. 357–375). Washington, DC: American Psychological Association.

Healy, K., Smith, C., & O'Sullivan, C. (1998). *Batterer intervention: Program approaches and criminal justice strategies.* Washington, DC: National Institute of Justice.

Henry, W., Schacht, T., & Strupp, H. (1986). Structural analysis of social behavior: Application to a study of interpersonal process in differential psychotherapeutic outcome. *Journal of Consulting and Clinical Psychology, 54,* 27–31.

Henry, W., Schacht, T., & Strupp, H. (1990). Patient and therapist introject, interpersonal process, and differential psychotherapy outcome. *Journal of Consulting and Clinical Psychology, 58,* 768–774.

Holtzworth-Munroe, A. (1992). Social skill deficits in maritally violent men: Interpreting the data using a social information processing model. *Clinical Psychology Review, 12*(6), 605–617.

Holtzworth-Munroe, A., & Hutchinson, G. (1993). Attributing negative intent to wife behavior: The attributions of maritally violent versus nonviolent men. *Journal of Abnormal Psychology, 102*(2), 206–11.

Holtzworth-Munroe, A. & Stuart, G. (1994). Typologies of male batterers: Three subtypes and the differences among them. *Psychological Bulletin, 116,* 476–497.

Hotaling, G., & Sugarman, D. (1986). An analysis of risk markers in husband to wife violence: The current state of knowledge. *Violence and Victims, 1,* 101–124.

Jacobson, N., & Gottman, J. (1998a, Mar/Apr). Anatomy of a violent relationship. *Psychology Today, 31*(2), 60–84.

Jacobson, N., & Gottman, J. (1998b). *When men batter women.* New York: Simon & Schuster.

Johnson, M. (1995). Patriarchal terrorism and common couple violence: Two forms of violence against women. *Journal of Marriage and the Family, 57,* 283–294.

Kalmuss, D. (1984). The intergenerational transmission of marital aggression. *Journal of Marriage and the Family, 46,* 11–19.

Kiley, D. (1983). *The Peter Pan syndrome*. New York: Avon.

Kivel, P. (1992). *Men's Work: How to Stop the Violence That Tears Our Lives Apart*. New York: Ballantine.

Lange, A. J., & Jakubowski, P. (1976). *Responsible assertive behavior: Cognitive/behavioral procedures for trainers*. Champaign, IL: Research Press.

Lee, M., Greene, G., Uken, A., Rheinscheld, L., & Sebold, J. (1997, June 29–July 2). *Solution-focused brief treatment: A viable modality for treating domestic violence offenders?* Paper presented at the 5th International Family Violence Research Conference, Durham, NH.

Lindsey, M., McBride, R. W., & Platt, C. M. (1993). *Amend: Philosophy and curriculum for treating batterers*. Littleton, CO: Gylantic Publishing.

McKay, M., Rogers, P. D., & McKay, J. (1989). *When anger hurts: Quieting the storm within*. Oakland, CA: New Harbinger.

Meichenbaum, D. (1977). *Cognitive-behavior modification: An integrative approach*. New York: Plenum.

Murphy, C., & Baxter, V. (1997). Motivating batterers to change in the treatment context. *Journal of Interpersonal Violence, 12*(4), 607–619.

Neidig, P. H. & Friedman, D. H. (1984). *Spouse abuse: A treatment program for couples*. Champaign, IL: Research Press.

Novaco, R. (1975). *Anger control: The development and evaluation of an experimental treatment*. Lexington, MA: Lexington Books.

Novaco, R. (1978). Anger and coping with stress: Cognitive behavioral interventions. In J. P. Foreyt and D. P. Rathjen (Eds.), *Cognitive behavior therapy: Research and applications*. New York: Plenum.

Novaco, R. (1979). The cognitive regulation of anger and stress. In P. Kendall & S. Hollon (Eds.), *Cognitive-behavioral interventions: Theory, research and procedure*. New York: Academic Press.

O'Leary, K. D. (1988). Physical aggression between spouses: A social learning perspective. In V. B. Van Hasselt, R. L. Morrison, A. S. Bellack, & M. Hersen (Eds.), *Handbook of Family Violence*. New York: Plenum.

O'Hanlon, W., & Weiner-Davis, M. (1989). *In search of solutions*. New York: Norton.

Pence, E. (1987). *In our best interest: A process for personal and social change*. Duluth: Minnesota Program Development, Inc.

Pence, E., & Paymar, M. (1993). *Education groups for men who batter: The Duluth model*. New York: Springer.

Pleck, J. (1980). Men's power with women, other men and society. In E. Pleck & J. Pleck (Eds.), *The American man* (pp. 417–433). Englewood Cliffs, NJ: Prentice-Hall.

Prince, J., & Arias, I. (1994). The role of perceived control and the desirability of control among abusive and nonabusive husbands. *American Journal of Family Therapy, 22*(2), 126–134.

Prochaska, J. O., & DiClemente, C. C. (1992). *The transtheoretical approach. Handbook of psychotherapy integration* (pp. 300–334). New York: Basicbooks.

Rose, S. D. (1989). *Working with adults in groups: Integrating cognitive-behavioral and small group strategies*. San Francisco: Jossey-Bass.

Russell, M. N. & Frohberg, J. (1995). *Confronting abusive beliefs: Group treatments for abusive men*. Thousand Oaks, CA: Sage.

Saunders, D. G. (1982). Counseling the violent husband. In P. Keller & L. Ritt (Eds.), *Innovations in clinical practice: A source book, Vol. I*. Sarasota, FL: Professional Resource Exchange.

Saunders, D. G. (1984). Helping husbands who batter. *Social Casework, 65,* 347–356.

Saunders, D. G. (1994). Prediction of wife assault. In J. C. Campbell (Ed), *Assessing dangerousness: Violence by sexual offenders, batterers, and child abusers*. Newbury Park, CA: Sage.

Saunders, D. G. (1996a). Interventions for men who batter. Do we know what works? *In session: Psychotherapy in practice, 2*(3), 81–94.

Saunders, D. G. (1996b). Feminist-cognitive-behavioral and process-psychodynamic treatments for men who batter: Interaction of abuser traits and treatment models. *Violence and Victims, 11*(4), 393–413.

Saunders, D. G., & Azar, S. (1989). Family violence treatment programs: Description and evaluation. In L. Ohlin & M. Tonry (Eds.), *Crime and violence: Special volume on family violence.*

Saunders, D. G., & Browne (1991). Domestic Homicide. In R. Ammerman & M. Hersen (Eds.), *Case studies in family violence.* New York: Plenum.

Saunders, D. G., & Browne, A. (in press). Intimate partner homicide. In R. Ammerman and M. Hersen (Eds.), *Case studies in family violence.* NY: Plenum.

Schecter, S. & Ganley, A. (1995). *Domestic violence: A national curriculum for family preservation practitioners.* San Francisco: Family Violence Prevention Fund.

Shapiro, S. (1995). *Talking with patients: A self psychological view.* Northvale, NJ: Aronson.

Sonkin, D., & Durphy, M. (1989). *Learning to live without violence.* Volcano, CA: Volcano Press.

Steinfeld, G. J. (1986). Spouse abuse: Clinical implications of research on the control of aggression. *Journal of Family Violence, 1*(2), 197–208.

Stoltenberg, J. (1993). *The end of manhood: A book for men of conscience.* New York: Dutton.

Stordeur, R. A., & Stille, R. (1989). *Ending men's violence against their partners.* Thousand Oaks, CA: Sage.

Stosny, S. (1995). *Treating attachment abuse.* NY: Springer.

Straus, M. A., & Gelles, R. J. (1990). *Physical violence in American families: Risk factors and adaptations to violence in 8,145 families.* New Brunswick, NJ: Transaction Press.

Straus, M., Gelles, R., and Steinmetz, S. (1980). *Behind closed doors: Violence in the American family.* Garden City, NY: Doubleday.

Tolman, R. M. (1996). Expanding sanctions for batterers: What can we do besides jailing and counseling them? In J. L. Edleson & Z. C. Eisikovits (Eds.). *Future interventions with battered women and their families.* Thousand Oaks, CA: Sage.

Tolman, R. M., & Edleson, J. L. (1995). Intervention for men who batter: A review of research. In S. Stith & M. A. Straus (Eds.), *Understanding partner violence* (pp. 262–274). Minneapolis: National Council on Family Relations.

Wachter, O., & Boyd, T. (1982). Time out. In M. Roy (Ed.), *The abusive partner: An analysis of domestic battering.* New York: Van Nostrand Reinhold.

Walker, L. (1984). *The battered woman syndrome.* New York: Springer.

Weiss, J., & Sampson, H. (1986). *The psychoanalytic process.* New York: Guilford.

Wexler, D. (1991). *The adolescent self: Strategies for self-management, self-soothing, and self-esteem in adolescence.* New York: Norton.

Wexler, D. (1991b). *The Prism Workbook.* New York: Norton.

Wexler, D. (1994). *Controlling "uncontrollable" behavior.* Unpublished article, Relationship Violence Training Institute, San Diego, CA.

White, M., & Weiner, M. (1986). *The theory and practice of self psychology.* New York: Brunner/Mazel.

Williams, O. J. (1995). Treatment for African American men who batter. *CURA Reporter, 25,* 6–10.

Williams, O. J., & Becker, R. L. (1994). Domestic partner abuse treatment programs and cultural competence: The results of a national survey. *Violence and Victims, 9*(3), 287–296.

Wolf, E. (1988). *Treating the self: Elements of clinical self psychology.* New York: Guilford.

Wolfe, B. (1989). Heinz Kohut's self psychology: A conceptual analysis. *Psychotherapy, 26,* 545–554.

Young, J. E. (1990). Cognitive therapy for personality disorders: A schema-focused approach. Sarasota, FL: Professional Resource Exchange.

INDEX

abuse
  child, as a form of spouse abuse, 45–46
  connection with alcohol and other substance
    use, 73
  physical, defining in group therapy, 44
  social isolation as, 45
  see also emotional abuse
abusers
  attachment, 8
  spouse, subtypes, 10–11
accountability
  Session 14, 109–11
  for violent behavior, 24–25
accusations, 145
active listening, Session 20, 136–40
aggression
  components of, 26
  defining, 123
  means of intimidation, 45
  red flags, Session 3, 59–63
  by Type I male spouse abusers, 10
alcohol, Session 5, 71–75
Amherst H. Wilder Foundation, 10, 20, 89
anger
  aggression stemming from, 26–27
  averting aggression in, 51
  red flags, Session 3, 59–63
  self-talk for coping with, Session 7, 81–85
  self-talk that produces, examples, 80
  in Type I male spouse abusers, 10
  warning signs of, 60
  ways to understand, 61–62
anger ladder, 26, 85, 93
  example, 82
  using in group sessions, 94
Anger Ladder, audiotape, xiv, 93, 94
argument, problem-solving versus battling with, 154
Arias, I., 9
arousal reduction, in behavioral therapy, 25–26

assertiveness
  in accepting compliments, 151
  defining, 123
  Session 17, 121–25
  teaching to a passive male, 28–29
  training in, 23
attachment abusers, 8
attack
  examples of mind games involving coercion, 48
  to meet criticism, 133–34
  see also aggression
attitudes, inner conflict with core values, 22
audiotape, *see Anger Ladder; Brief Quieting Reflex;*
    Quieting Reflex
awfulizing, example of "bad rap," 78

Babcock, J., 10
bad rap, Session 6, 76–80
Bandura, A., 23
batterers
  Type II male spouse abusers as, 10–11
  typology of, 9–13
Baxter, V., 14, 15
Beck, A. T., 27, 28
Becker, R. L., 31
Bedrosian, R. C., 27
behavioral approaches, 22–23
behavior problems, in kids whose parents fight,
    171
beliefs
  inner conflict of attitudes with core values, 22
  irrational, leading to anger, 26–27
black and white, example of "bad rap," 78
blackouts, as a symptom of severe alcohol abuse, 72
blaming
  erroneous, aspect of a bad rap, 78
  examples of mind games involving, 48
bonding, in a group session, 88–89
borderline personality, of Type III batterers, 11
Boyd, T., 100

brainstorming, for problem solutions, 155
Brannen, S. J., 30
Brief Quieting Reflex, audiotape, xiv, 64, 71
Browne, A., 21, 31
Browne, K., 18, 22, 30

Carrillo, R., 31
change
    asking for, Session 18, 126–29
    transfer of, 186–88
child abuse, as a form of spouse abuse, 45–46
classical conditioning, 26
client-centered approaches, xiii
    group formats, 18–20
    respect in, 15–20
clinical tips, 3–5
coercion
    examples of mind games involving, 48
    force in sexual abuse, 164
    threat, physiological responses to, 52
cognitive approaches, 22, 23, 26–28
    evaluation of, 29
common couple violence, 9
communication
    destructive patterns in, 143
    by kids, 177
    see also listening
compassion, HEALS technique using, 83
Compassion Workshop, 19
compliments, Session 23, 149–51
conflict, respectful, Session 24, 152–57
confrontation
    culturally appropriate use of, 31
    treatment based on, effects, 14–15
contempt, 145–46
contingency management, 23–25
control, examples of mind games involving, 49
control-mastery theory, 14
    House of Abuse metaphor for, 46
coping techniques
    for anger, self-talk, 81–85
    lack of, in batterers, 27
core values, inner conflict with attitudes, 22
costs, of aggression, 24
cotherapists, male and female team, 4
countertransference, issues in, overidentification with
        the perpetrator, 20
couples approach, counterindications, 22
criticism, 145
    handling, Session 19, 130–35
cue therapy, 182–83
cultural competence, of therapy programs, 31
cycles
    of abuse, Session 4, 64–67
    Cycle of Feeling Avoidance, 17–18
    Cycle of Intolerable Feelings, 91, 93
    Cycle of Violence, 17

decision-making
    egalitarian, teaching in therapy, 28–29
    responsibility for, 156

defenses, accountability, 110–11
defensiveness, 145–46
    in response to compliments, 151
Deffenbacher, J. L., 25
denial
    in the cycle of abuse, 67
    meeting criticism with, 132
dependent personalities, therapy for batterers with, 30
DiClemente, C. C., 31
Dinkmeyer, D., 176, 179
down-putting, example of "bad rap," 78, *see also*
        put-downs
Duluth model, of intervention, 13
Durphy, M., 23, 24–25
Dutton, D., 8, 11–13, 15, 22, 28, 106, 108, 136–37
DV2000 Resources for Men, xiv
D'Zurilla, T., 27

Eddy, M. J., 23
Edleson, J. L., 22, 23, 26, 30
education, as treatment, Duluth model, 13
effectiveness, of treatment, studies of, 30
Ellis, A., 26, 27
emergency strategy, time-out as, 54
EMERGE program, Boston, 31
emotional abuse
    defining in group therapy, 44–45
    examples of mind games involving, 48
    problems in kids whose parents fight, 171
emotional reasoning, example of "bad rap," 78
empathy training, Session 21, 141–42
entitlement
    changing a sense of, 22
    examining aspects of, xiii
    male, and patriarchal violence, 9
    rights as a man, 100
    see also privilege
equality
    in decision-making, teaching in therapy, 28–29
    and self-respect, 158
Equality Wheel, 161
Erickson, M., 3, 15
error in blaming, example of "bad rap," 78
evaluation
    of cognitive and behavioral approaches, 29
    form for, 37
Evans, K., 17, 19, 91, 93
excuse-making
    to meet criticism, 133
    using alcohol for, 72
explanation, HEALS technique, 83
explosion, in the cycle of abuse, 67
expressive power, of women, 7
extinction, time-out technique for inducing, 23

Fagan, J., 24
fairness, in conflict with respect, 154
family
    conflict in, and spouse abuse by children as
        adults, 12

locus of abuse, for Type II batterers, 10–11
put-downs from parents, 108
fear
   and intimidation, 45
   in kids whose parents fight, 171
   recounting an incident of fright, 183–84
feelings
   common, classifying by primary type, 92
   expressing
      Session 18, 126–29
      Session 20, 136–40
   "the Feelings List," HEALS technique, 83
   managing, Session 9, 90–93
   primary, 91
feminist approaches, 22, 29–30
Fischer, G., 14
force, in sexual abuse, 164
forms
   evaluation, 37
   key, xiv
   men's group, 38–39
   orientation, 38–39
   weekly check-in, 35–36
Foundations for Violence-Free Living, 20
"The Four Horsemen of the Apocalypse," Session 22,
   143–48
fragmentation of men, effect of deficient mirroring, 7
Freeman, A., 28
freeze-frame approach, 16
fright, recounting an incident of, 183–84
Frohberg, J., 22
frustration, expressed in violence, 9

Ganley, A., 23, 55, 172–73
gaslighting defense, 145–46
Geffner, R., 61–62, 63, 124, 132, 155
Gelles, R. J., 13, 21
gender, and sources of violent behavior, 21–22
Gilligan, S., 15
Golant, S., 8, 11–13, 22, 106, 136–37
Goldfried, M., 27
Gondolf, E. W., 28, 30
Gottman, J., 10, 13–14, 18, 19, 65, 143, 145,
   147–48
Greene, G., 20
grieving, of childhood losses, in therapy, 18–19
group
   open-ended format for, xiii
   orientation form, 38–39

Hamberger, L. K., 21
Hare, R., 10
Harway, M., 17, 19, 91, 93
healing, HEALS technique, 83
HEALS technique, 19, 81, 83
Healy, K., 31
Henry, W., 14
Holtzworth-Munroe, A., 10, 17, 23, 28, 105
homework, time-out technique, 52
honeymoon phase, following violence, 65

Hotaling, G., 13, 22
House of Abuse
   the room of sexual abuse in, 164
   Session 1, 43–49
House of Self-Worth & Empowerment, 87, 89
Hutchinson, G., 17, 105

"I" messages, 129
intentions, negative, 105
interpretation
   misattribution by abusive men, 17–18
   misinterpretations and jealousy, 101–5
   and resultant self-talk, 76–77
interrupting, by parents, 178
interventions
   group, for male batterers, 21–31
   power and control based, 13
intimidation, means of, 45
isolation, examples of mind games involving, 48

Jacobson, N., 10, 13–14, 65
Jakubowski, P., 28
jealousy
   example, Joe, 103–4
   Session 12, 101–5
   as terror of abandonment, 8
Johnson, M., 9, 13, 17

Kalmuss, D., 13
kids
   asking opinion of, 178
   courtesy by, 177
   examples for discussion, 173
   Session 27, 169–73
   symptoms in, when parents fight, 171
Kiley, D., 167–68
Kivel, P., 30

Lange, A. J., 28
language, personal meaning constructed through,
   19–20
La Taillade, J., 10
leading, *see* pacing and leading
Lee, M., 20
legal system, use of, and success of treatment, 31
limitations
   in new skill implementation, 5
   in use of the manual, xiv
Lindsey, M., 30, 114–15
listening
   active, Session 20, 136–40
   to kids, 176
   by kids, 177
   by parents, 178
love, HEALS technique, 83

McBride, R. W., 30
McGrane, M. F., 47
McKay, G., 176, 179

McKay, J., 26
McKay, M., 26
McNamara, K., 25
maladaptive schemas, from childhood trauma, 28
male privilege, *see* entitlement; privilege
Mantooth, C., 61–62, 63, 124, 132, 155
marriage, expectations of, 157, 158–61
masculinity traps I, Session 10, 94–96
masculinity traps II, Session 11, 97–100
masculinity traps: sex, 165
masculinity-validating power, of women, 7
Meichenbaum, D., 22, 26, 27
men
    culturally appropriate choice of therapy approach
        for, 31
    fragmentation of, 7
    resources for, xiv
men's group, forms, 38–39
mind games
    examples, 48–49
    as sexual abuse, 164
mindreading, example of "bad rap," 78
minimizing, example of "bad rap," 78
mirror, broken, 6–20
mirroring selfobject, 6, 16–18
misattribution, by abusive men, 17–18
misinterpretations, and jealousy, 101–5
modeling
    by group leaders, of a serious tone, 4
    for learning new behavior, 28–29
    to teach responsible assertive behavior, 23
    see also pacing and leading
mother, source of self-cohesion, 6
Murphy, C., 14, 15
Myers, T., 23

narcissistic injury, vulnerability to, 17
narcissistic rage, 7–8
Native American culture, and choice of therapy
        approach, 31
Nine Commandments, 4, 53, 109
    introducing, 50–51
Novaco, R., 26, 84

Oakland Men's Project, 29–30
O'Hanlon, W., 19
O'Leary, K. D., 23
open-ended group format, xiii
orientation form, group, 38–39
O'Sullivan, C., 31

pacing and leading
    clinical strategy of, 3–4, 15–16
    model for managing feelings, 159
parents
    abusive, 7–8
    father
        effect of rejection by, 106–7
        result of shaming by, 12–13
    mother, attachment to, 12–13
    Session 28, 174–79

partners
    culturally appropriate choice of therapy approach
        for, 51
    information about time-out techniques for, 51,
        55–56
    managing in blocked time-out departures, 57
passive-aggressive behavior, defining, 123
passive behavior, defining, 123
patriarchal terrorism, 9
    as a source of violence, 13–14
Paymar, M., 13, 29, 111, 118, 156
peers, role in preserving change, 186
Pence, E., 13, 29, 111, 118, 156
people problems, in kids whose parents fight, 171
personality/personality disorders, 28
    borderline personality, 11
    dependent personality, 30
physical abuse
    defining in group therapy, 44
    and sexual abuse, 164
physical effects
    of alcohol, and abusive behavior, 72
    physiological responses to threat, 52
planning, by kids, 177
Platt, C. M., 30
Pleck, J., 7, 18–19
positive reinforcement, for developing skills
        incompatible with aggression, 24–25
Potente, T., 21
power
    masculinity-validating, of women, 7
    struggles over, with new group members, 4
Power and Control Wheel, 160
powerlessness, and responsibility, 5
pressure, as sexual abuse, 164
Prevention Plan I, Session 31, 185–87
Prevention Plan II, Session 32, 188–91
Prince, J., 9
privilege
    examining aspects of, xiii
    male
        abusive claim of, 45
        examples of mind games involving, 49
    see also entitlement
problems, ownership of, 179
problem-solving, 27
    HEALS technique, 83
    Session 24, 152–57
process psychodynamic treatment, 18–19
Prochaska, J. O., 31
progressive relaxation, 25
psychological abuse
    correlation with patriarchal terrorism, 9
    defining in group therapy, 44–45
    and sexual abuse, 164
put-downs
    examples of mind games involving, 48
    from parents, 108
    Session 13, 106–8
    as sexual abuse, 164

questionnaires
　　alcohol and other substance abuse, 74
　　put-downs from parents, 108
　　rape, 167–68
　　sexual meaning, 166
Quieting Reflex, xiv, 60

rape
　　guilt over, 167–68
　　"I Raped My Wife" (patient's story), 167–68
rational emotive therapy, 22, 26–27
reasons, for substance use, 75
Reavis, J. A., 136, 186
refusal, assertive, examples, 128
rehearsal
　　for learning new behaviors, 28–29
　　Switch! technique for, 112–16
　　to teach responsible assertive behavior, 23
relationships, adult, remedying imperfect mirroring
　　in, 7
relaxation training, 23, 59–60
　　audiotapes used for, xiv
　　progressive relaxation, 25
　　see also Brief Quieting Reflex; The Quieting Reflex
religion, abusive use of, 45
remorse
　　in the cycle of abuse, 67
　　by Type II batterers, 10–11
repair mechanisms, to restore mutual respect, 148
requests, assertive, examples, 128
resistance, initial, 4
resources, xiv
respect
　　in client-centered approaches, 15–20
　　conflict with, 152–57
　　for men in the program, 3
　　repair mechanisms to restore, 148
responses
　　to criticism
　　　　constructive, 133–34
　　　　destructive, 132–33
　　see also active listening; communication
responsibility
　　the 100% rule, 44
　　for behavior while drunk, 72
　　for decisions, fixing, 156
　　plan for time-outs, 58
　　see also Nine Commandments
rewards, of aggression, 23–24
Rheinscheld, L., 20
rights as a man, 100
Rogers, P. D., 26
Rose, S. D., 28
Rossi, E., 15
Rubin, A., 30
Rushe, R., 10
Russell, D. M., 30
Russell, M. N., 22

Sabadell, P. M., 25
Sampson, H., 14

Saunders, D. G., 16, 18, 21, 22, 23, 24, 26, 28, 30,
　　31, 59, 80, 85, 96, 103
Schacht, T., 14
Schecter, S., 55, 172–73
Sebold, J., 20
self-cohesion
　　generating, 7
　　need for, 18
　　　　source in the mother, 6
　　regaining with sense of power, 8
self-disclosure, by a therapist, 5
self-esteem
　　maintaining in therapy, 14
　　maintaining with appreciation, 8
　　Session 8, 86–89
selfobject
　　of the perpetrator, validity of, 8
　　self psychological approach, 16–18
selfobject figures, regard of others only as, 18
self psychological approach, xiii
　　for treating relationship violence, 6–20
self-respect, and equality, 158
self-talk
　　for anger management, 84
　　confident, Session 15, 112–16
　　dangerous, Session 15, 112–16
　　example, 118
　　masculinity trap, 95, 97–100
　　pacing and leading example, 4
　　parents' patterns of, 175
　　Session 6, 76–80
sex, Session 26, 162–68
sexual abuse, 45
　　defined, 162
Sexual Meaning Questionnaire, 166
shame, 11–13
　　being subjected to in childhood, 107
　　as an element of confrontational therapy, 14–15
Shapiro, S., 6, 9, 16
Shortt, J., 10
skills integration, Session 16, 117–18
sleep problems, in kids whose parents fight, 171
Smith, C., 31
social competence, of Type III batterers, 11
social isolation, as a form of abuse, 45
social learning theory, 23
　　about chemical abuse and aggression, 72
sociocultural model, confronting abuse in,
　　13–14
solution-focused therapy, 19–20, *see also*
　　problem-solving
Sonkin, D., 23, 24–25
spouse abuse, subtypes of, 10–11
Staeker, K., 18, 22, 30
stages of change approach, 31
Stark, R. S., 25
Steinfeld, G. J., 24
Steinmetz, S., 13
Stille, R., 22, 23, 30
Stoltenberg, J., 30
stonewalling, 145–46

Stordeur, R. A., 22, 23, 30
Stosny, S., 8, 13, 19, 22, 83
Straus, M. A., 13, 21
Strazomski, A., 106, 108
stress inoculation therapy, 22
Strupp, H., 14
Stuart, G., 10, 28
substance abuse, Session 5, 71–75
Sugarman, D., 13, 22
Switch!, a rehearsal technique, 112
systematic desensitization, 26
system-bashing, in groups, strategy for meeting, 5

taking time, by parents, 177
teasing, abusive, 44
Tello, J., 31
tension building, in the cycle of abuse, 67
therapists
    empathic, success of, 14–15
    "one-down" position of, solution-focused
        therapy, 20
    problems of, in treating personality disorders, 28
    self-disclosure by, 5
therapy programs, *see* treatment
threat, physiological responses to, 52
time machine technique, 188–89
time-out technique
    in behavioral treatment, 24–25
    Session 2, 50–58
    versus stonewalling, 146
Tolman, R. M., 22, 23, 24, 26, 30
Transfer of Change, 189–91
transition, prevention plan II, 188
treatment
    behavioral approaches, 22–23
    client-centered approaches, xiii, 15–20
    control-mastery theory, 14, 46
    cultural competence of therapy programs, 31
    Duluth model, 13
    effectiveness of, studies, 30
    EMERGE program, Boston, 31
    evaluation of cognitive and behavioral
        approaches, 29
    failure of
        confrontation about, 5
        for Type I "cobra" abusers, 10

feminist approaches, xiii, 22
HEALS technique, 19, 81, 83
process psychodynamic approaches, 18–19
self psychological model, xiii, 6–20
solution-focused, 19–20
stages of change approach, 31

Uken, A., 20

van Ginkel, C., 106, 108
verbal abuse, defining in group therapy, 44–45
videotapes
    Compassion, 81
    The Great Santini, 95, 107, 136, 169
    Men's Work, 97–98
violence
    appropriate alternatives to, 62
    common couple, 9
    danger of, profiles, 31
    family, stages in, 64
    relationship, self psychological treatment
        perspective for, 6–20
    Session 29 and 30, 183–84
volatility, of Type III batterers, 11

Wachter, O., 100
Walker, L., 17, 21, 66
Waltz, J., 10
weekly check-in, forms for, 35–36
Weiner, M., 7, 9, 16
Weiner-Davis, M., 19
Weiss, J., 14
Wexler, D., 16, 76, 78–79, 187
White, M., 7, 9, 16
Williams, O. J., 31
withdrawal ritual, to prevent violence, 65
Wolf, E., 16
Wolfe, B., 16
women
    objectification of, in groups, 30
    perceived superiority of, and male dependence on,
        18–19
    power of, 7
women-bashing, in groups, confronting, 4–5

Young, J. E., 28